# PRAISE FOR
# *MERE SEXUALITY*

*Mere Sexuality* is a faithful, readable navigation through questions of sexuality, pointing toward the gospel and our truest identity as sons and daughters in Christ. In our sexually confused times, this book has clarity and conviction.

RUSSELL MOORE, PRESIDENT OF THE ETHICS AND RELIGIOUS LIBERTY COMMISSION OF THE SOUTHERN BAPTIST CONVENTION

Todd Wilson has given us a thoughtful, sensitive, and, above all, deeply Christian book about sexual morality and marriage. It brings into the foreground the power and beauty of the biblical understanding of marriage as a truly conjugal bond—a joining of hearts and minds, yes, but one founded upon the biological union made possible by the sexual-reproductive complementarity of male and female. Pastor Wilson shows us that the Christian "no" to sexual sins is rooted in the profound Christian "yes" to the goodness of truly conjugal union.

ROBERT P. GEORGE, MCCORMICK PROFESSOR OF JURISPRUDENCE AT PRINCETON UNIVERSITY

Todd Wilson offers an orthodox, holistic, and compassionate treatment of this most powerful, perplexing, and delightful gift from God. *Mere Sexuality* is exceptional, not only in offering a compelling argument for God's ideal for human sexuality, but also in addressing with pastoral understanding and care the ways we fall short.

KAREN SWALLOW PRIOR, AUTHOR OF *BOOKED: LITERATURE IN THE SOUL OF ME* AND *FIERCE CONVICTIONS: THE EXTRAORDINARY LIFE OF HANNAH MORE—POET, REFORMER, ABOLITIONIST*

We need this book! In our highly sexualized culture, we need careful reflection, both theologically and with the practical challenges in view. Todd Wilson gives us just that—and with a wise and gracious spirit. This is a must-read for scholars, pastors, and others who want solid guidance on the issues.

RICHARD J. MOUW, PHD, PRESIDENT EMERITUS, PROFESSOR OF FAITH AND PUBLIC LIFE, FULLER THEOLOGICAL SEMINARY

The human sexual union is of utmost importance in the Judeo-Christian tradition. It is the first act God gave humanity to get busy with. Unfortunately, the Christian church has lost its way on the topic, influenced by the world just as much as, if not more than, by the teaching of God's Word. Todd Wilson aims to put this right, and *Mere Sexuality* is a major contribution to this essential effort. It is faithfully biblical, helpfully practical, and immensely thoughtful. Every serious Christian should read and benefit from Wilson's wisdom here.

GLENN T. STANTON, DIRECTOR OF FAMILY FORMATION STUDIES AT FOCUS ON THE FAMILY AND AUTHOR OF *LOVING MY (LGBT) NEIGHBOR*

In *Mere Sexuality*, Todd Wilson takes on the challenge of articulating Christian norms regarding sex and gender. He does so in a clear, accessible way. Followers of Christ will be indebted to Wilson for helping us identify and articulate those norms in a dramatically changing culture in which such norms are all but lost.

MARK A. YARHOUSE, PsyD, PROFESSOR OF PSYCHOLOGY & HUGHES ENDOWED CHAIR; DIRECTOR OF THE INSTITUTE FOR THE STUDY OF SEXUAL IDENTITY AT REGENT UNIVERSITY

Yeats probably did not have sexuality in mind when he penned his famous poetic line "things fall apart; the center cannot hold," but he may as well have, for sexual anarchy has indeed been loosed upon the world. Todd Wilson brings Christian clarity and charity to the confusion, reminding the church of what it has known for nearly two thousand years but recently forgotten: *mere sexuality*, the historic consensus that God created human beings male and female as part of a larger design plan for union and communion, and that human flourishing depends on our respecting, not disrespecting, this created order, an order that is enabling, not disabling. The book provides rich resources for pastors and others seeking wisdom on this issue, but the chapter on Jesus' sexuality especially stood out as "merely" breathtaking.

KEVIN J. VANHOOZER, RESEARCH PROFESSOR OF SYSTEMATIC THEOLOGY AT TRINITY EVANGELICAL DIVINITY SCHOOL

Years ago, in the midst of a world war, an incredibly timely and now timeless book came out called *Mere Christianity*. Today, I have the honor of recommending to you *Mere Sexuality*. This is a *crucial* book for you to read *now* amidst our exploding culture wars. Todd Wilson writes in a way that pushes back hatred and anger. He lays out a case for biblical sexuality that is simply unmatched in its clarity and insight for those seeking truth and wisdom in this area. Don't hide from this topic and think it will go away. Dig into this short, powerful book, and be encouraged that you can hold firm to your faith and still walk with and love others well.

JOHN TRENT, PhD, CHAPMAN CHAIR OF MARRIAGE AND FAMILY
MINISTRY AND THERAPY AT MOODY THEOLOGICAL SEMINARY

This is not just another book about sex; it is a tract for the times. Relevant, timely, and theologically rich, it connects sexuality with Christology and offers practical pastoral wisdom on a topic that God cares about a lot. Strongly recommended!

TIMOTHY GEORGE; FOUNDING DEAN OF BEESON DIVINITY
SCHOOL OF SAMFORD UNIVERSITY; GENERAL EDITOR OF
THE *REFORMATION COMMENTARY ON SCRIPTURE*

# MERE SEXUALITY

# MERE SEXUALITY

## REDISCOVERING THE CHRISTIAN VISION OF SEXUALITY

## TODD WILSON

ZONDERVAN

*Mere Sexuality*
Copyright © 2017 by Todd A. Wilson

This title is also available as a Zondervan ebook.

Requests for information should be addressed to:
Zondervan, *3900 Sparks Dr. SE, Grand Rapids, Michigan 49546*

ISBN 978-0-310-53535-5

*Cover design: brandnavigation.com*
*Cover image: Shutterstock.com*
*Interior design: Denise Froehlich*

*Printed in the United States of America*

HB 02.06.2019

*To Wesley Hill—*

ἐπιστολὴ Χριστοῦ

# CONTENTS

# THE ROAD AHEAD

In recent years, many people have written about same-sex practice and gay marriage, and much of this material is quite good. Evangelicals have grappled with the biblical texts that speak to the issue of same-sex practice. They've written books, both academic and popular, and we should be thankful for their labor of love. A number of authors have also helped us hear the stories of those who are same-sex-attracted and think about how we might treat them not as an issue to be solved, but as people to be loved. So whether or not you affirm same-sex relationships, we can agree that these signs are encouraging. The church is taking Scripture and its application seriously, and we should feel good about that.

So you may wonder why I felt the need to add yet another book to the mix. Here's why: I don't think we've dealt adequately with the question of homosexuality in the light of God's design for human sexuality. Instead, we've addressed the issue too narrowly—at times almost exclusively in biblical or personal and practical terms. What do I mean? Our approach has been to ask one of two questions—a biblical question or a personal and practical question: What does the Bible really teach about homosexuality? Or, How can we love homosexuals as Jesus would?[1] Of course, these are important questions, but they're not the only questions we should ask. They're not sufficient to settle the issue of what we should think about same-sex relationships. We need to put the question in a larger theological context.

And that's what I try to do in this book. The issues we explore here go beyond questions of same-sex practice, gay marriage, or how to love homosexuals the way Jesus would. We'll touch on a whole range of biblical, theological, cultural, and practical questions related to human sexuality—from birth control and transgenderism to the hook-up culture and theologian Karl Barth's view of the image of God.

In chapter 1, I introduce the idea of "mere sexuality"— what it is and why it matters. Did you know that, despite a genuine diversity of views expressed along the way, the church has held to a coherent vision of human sexuality for centuries? Given the fractured state of evangelical Christianity today, it's easy to forget that there is a historic Christian consensus on same-sex practice and gay marriage—and that Christians in centuries past had good reasons to support this consensus. We'll explore what these are in chapter 1.

In chapter 2, we'll take a careful look at Jesus and his sexuality. For many, Jesus' sexuality is a foreign concept. But his sexuality is crucial for how we understand our sexuality. We need to take a long, hard look at not only what Jesus thought or taught about sexuality, but also at who Jesus was and is as a full-fledged human and thus a sexual being. Let's not forget: Jesus has armpit hair, male hormones, a Y chromosome, and all the rest that is common to male sexuality. What does any of this mean for how we think about human sexuality? We'll explore this in chapter 2.

Chapter 3 asks how our sexuality relates to our identity. As human beings, we have a strong tendency to link our identity with our sexuality. We have an intuitive sense that our sexuality is significant not just for personal recreation but for identity formation as well. And as we will see, there is good biblical reason for this connection. We'll take our point of departure from Genesis 1 and explore what it means to be created in the image of God as male and female.

In chapters 4 and 5, we turn our attention to the sensitive and controversial issues of the meaning of marriage and the purpose of sex. Scripture says that when a man and woman come together in the covenant of marriage, they form a "one flesh" union; that is, they form a union that is comprehensive. It involves heart, mind, and body. And this has profound implications for how we understand what constitutes marriage. But it also sheds light on how we ought to think about the purpose of sex, the topic we cover in chapter 5.

In chapter 6, we address perhaps the most difficult implication of mere sexuality, at least as it applies to same-sex-attracted people. Because mere sexuality authorizes sexual activity only within the context of marriage, understood as a one-flesh union between a man and a woman, same-sex-attracted people are often left with a difficult dilemma: either fall out of step with what the Bible and the church teach on sexuality, or confront the prospect of lifelong celibacy. But as we will show in this chapter, individual Christians and the Christian church can do much to redress this situation. We need to recover a biblical vision of friendship and strengthen the friendship culture of the church.

Chapter 7 considers how mere sexuality relates to eschatology and ethics, hope and holiness, our personal future and how we live in the present. We will see that there is a way of life that corresponds to mere sexuality, and it can be summarized in one simple word: patience. In fact, I will argue that patience is the key to living out the vision of mere sexuality faithfully.

In a final chapter, I encourage the church to do more than simply recover the lost vision of sexuality I articulate in this book. I call on Christians to cast vision for mere sexuality in their own spheres of influence. But we don't want to do this in a way that is overly muscular, ham-fisted, or insensitive. That won't accomplish the outcome we want. If mere sexuality will ever capture hearts and minds, we need to cast vision for it with joy, tears, and hope. This last chapter is my encouragement to pastors and teachers, parents and grandparents—really to anyone who cares about how to communicate these important truths to their friends and family or congregants and colleagues!

I'm sensitive to the fact that my strong emphasis on a

theological vision for human sexuality may lead some to conclude that what the Bible says is somehow secondary or less important. That would be a mistaken reading of this book. A theological vision is good only insofar as it reflects the Bible's vision, grounded in faithful exegesis of Scripture. Many fine scholars have done this work, and I won't imitate their efforts here.[2] But I wouldn't want to leave you with the impression that the vision of this book is only loosely connected to Scripture. So in a first appendix, I offer four core scriptural convictions that undergird the theological vision of this book.

Additionally, I wouldn't want anyone to assume that living out the Christian vision of human sexuality is pain-free. The reality is much different. Our lives are often messy, even our sexuality. We're broken people, deeply affected by the ravages of sin. Mere sexuality is often battered and bruised by brokenness. It becomes, in a sense, bent sexuality. We shouldn't shy away from this plain fact, even though it's a painful truth. I didn't want to in this book. So I included an appendix written by my friend Joel Willitts, who shares his own story of how sexual abuse (or "bent sexuality") has impacted his ability to embrace and live out mere sexuality. Joel's story is both potent and redemptive.

This book provides an introduction to the historic Christian vision of human sexuality, yet does so in conversation with this century's main challenges to that vision. And I hope that piques your interest! If you want a book that focuses on what the Bible says about homosexuality, then you should grab hold of the many excellent resources that do just that. But if you want to explore the Christian vision of human sexuality—a vision that, yes, speaks to homosexuality but also to a host of equally vital issues—then keep reading. There's something here for you.

## Different Types of Readers

People with different backgrounds, perspectives, and experiences will read this book, and because of these differences they'll respond to its message differently. This is the case with any book, but especially so with a book that addresses homosexuality. So let me take a moment to identify who you might be and how you might respond to what I've written.

You may be an *anxious observer*. You approach the issue of sexuality, and homosexuality in particular, much like the way you would watch your child ride a bike with no hands. Most, I suspect, fall in this first category. You're convinced of the Bible's teaching on sexuality, but you're anxious about what you see in the culture and the church. You don't wrestle with same-sex attraction or with the Bible's teaching on this issue. But you worry about how changes in the culture and the church will impact you and your children, grandchildren, workplace, neighborhood, and country. If that's you, I hope you gain confidence and wisdom from this book.

I can envision a second type of reader. Let's call this person a *sincere struggler*.[3] The sincere struggler is like the anxious observer in that you're convinced of what the Bible teaches about human sexuality. But you're different in that you wrestle with same-sex attraction and perhaps even same-sex practice. If this is you, I pray you will receive the message of this book as hope-filled good news—not necessarily easy news, but good news, because it holds a path toward human flourishing, contentment, and joy.

A third type of person is the *honest doubter.* You're someone who doubts the Bible's teaching on human sexuality, or at least what has often been thought of as the Bible's teaching. You're not sure what to make of the swirl of debate in the culture and the church over same-sex marriage. You've watched it unfold, and you feel torn. You may have been raised with a traditional view of things, but for a while now, you've had more questions than answers. If that's you, then I hope this book will bring you greater biblical clarity and conviction.

Some fall into a fourth category—the *genuine supporter.* You're someone who sympathizes with brothers and sisters in Christ who are same-sex-attracted. You may have a close friend, family member, or child who is same-sex-attracted, and you have worked hard to understand their situation. You may also be, by disposition, a compassionate person who finds it easy to empathize with people. And you may have studied this issue. Perhaps you picked up Justin Lee's *Torn* or Matthew Vines's *God and the Gay Christian*, and it has caused you to change your view on what the Bible teaches about homosexuality.[4] Now you support same-sex practice, at least in certain situations. If this describes you, then I hope this book encourages you in your love for those who experience same-sex attraction or identify as gay or lesbian, while at the same time giving you some important questions to wrestle with.

The final type of person I will address in the pages that follow is the *assertive advocate*. You are well settled in your convictions about the appropriateness of same-sex practice; as a result, you want to advocate for the Christian church to change its position on this issue. Assertive advocates could be either same-sex- or opposite-sex-attracted, Christian or not Christian. If that's you, then my hope is that you will find that this book takes your views seriously. At the same time, I hope this book will help you appreciate the historic Christian consensus on human sexuality so that you better understand the tradition from which you want to depart or distance yourself. Theologian Oliver O'Donovan put it well when he wrote, "No one who has not learned to be traditional can dare to innovate."[5]

Regardless of what type of reader you are, I hope this book both challenges and encourages you. All I would ask from you, regardless of which of the five types you most identify with, is that you stick with me through this book. If I say something that frustrates you, resist the temptation to throw it in the trash or let your dog chew it up. Keep reading to the end. Because only by coming to terms with the whole will you be in a position to make a responsible judgment.

## A Brief Word about Words (and Labels)

Here I should pause to say a few things about labels, because when we talk about homosexuality, labels matter. I recognize that one's choice of labels can be alienating to some and embracing of others. I'm sorry that's the case. I wish it weren't. Further, I recognize that labels carry deeper meanings and implications. And I'm sensitive to the pros and cons of different designations; in fact, I've gone round and round about which labels to use. I must confess that the old saw "damned if you do, damned if you don't" has come to mind on more than one occasion.

I have Christian friends who describe themselves as "gay," and I appreciate that they have good reasons for doing so.[6] I wouldn't fault anyone for using that term, as long as they're clear on its implications.[7] In this book, however, I've chosen to use the term "same-sex-attracted" rather than "gay." Again, I realize that both designations have drawbacks. But since this is a book about the Christian vision of human sexuality, I want to use terms that stress male and female as basic ontological categories and as normative for how we ought to think about human beings. Someone is male or female. But as a male or female, they may or may not experience same-sex attraction. That's why I've chosen, in most cases, to avoid the term "gay Christian."

Sam Allberry, a same-sex-attracted British pastor, puts it well, I think: "It sounds clunky to describe myself as 'someone who experiences same-sex attraction.' But describing myself like this is a way for me to recognize that the kind of sexual attractions I experience are not fundamental to my identity. They are part of *what I feel* but are not *who I am* in a fundamental sense. I am far more than my sexuality."[8] By choosing to speak of people as "same-sex-attracted" rather than as "gay," I mean no disrespect to those who identify that way. Nor do I intend to delegitimize anyone's experience. I only want to underscore the importance of sexual differentiation as basic to human existence and thereby reinforce the theological vision of sexuality you find in this book.

## My Prayer for This Book

I assume every Christian author begins a book project with desires and aspirations, hopes and prayers, for what God might be pleased to do through his word and by his Spirit in the lives of people. This is certainly true for this book and for me as its author.

My prayer for you as you read this book is that you will see the rational coherence of mere sexuality and be transfixed by its beauty. I pray that this book will instill in you renewed confidence in an old-fashioned Christian teaching. I pray that you will see its aesthetic and theological beauty, and that even if you remain unconvinced, you won't dismiss mere sexuality as narrow-minded, puritanical, or Pollyannaish.

My prayer is that you will welcome rather than resent your sexuality. There is a Manichean, dualistic, physical-bodies-are-bad mentality at work in the modern world—a view that biology, embodied sexuality, being male or female, is a limit to be overcome, a hindrance to be removed. Instead, this book will have achieved its goal if we view our sexuality, whether male or female, as a vocation to be embraced, a summons to sacrificial service for the good of others, a living out of our unique calling before God in this world.

My prayer is that this book will, by God's Spirit, bring about increased humility in the hearts of all of us who affirm what the Bible has to say about mere sexuality; in fact, that it will bring about deep repentance where necessary—a rejection of attitudes and actions that belittle those who struggle with their sexuality, whether heterosexual or homosexual.

My prayer is that this book will foster a climate within the evangelical church, and by extension in our homes and networks of relationships, where we can engage in honest, gracious, thoughtful conversation about sexuality and even homosexuality. The broader culture has lost its ability to do so. And sadly, so too has the church, which can often be either silent or bombastic, but in the end largely unhelpful.

And, finally, my prayer is for those who struggle with same-sex attraction. I pray that you will find strength to walk the path of my friend Wesley Hill. Wesley was a freshman at Wheaton College when I was there in graduate school. We became good friends. In fact, I mentored and loved him as an older brother. What I didn't know until later is that Wesley lives with same-sex attraction, and always has. He tells the story in his moving theological memoir, *Washed and Waiting:*

*Reflections on Christian Faithfulness and Homosexuality*. Wesley embraces the historic Christian view on same-sex practice and is therefore committed to a life of sexual chastity, which is not an easy road to walk. For Wesley, it means embracing the "confusion and sorrow and triumph and grief and joy of the struggle to live faithfully before God, in Christ, with others, as a gay person."[9] Wesley is walking this path well. And if that is your struggle, I pray that you will find the grace to do the same—and that this book will serve you in your journey.

# CHAPTER 1

# WHAT IS MERE SEXUALITY?

In June 2015, Ed Stetzer, executive director of the Billy Graham Center for Evangelism at Wheaton College, shared with the *New York Times* that the number of evangelicals who had come out in favor of same-sex marriage was so minimal "you could fit them all in an S.U.V."[1]

Today, I'm sure Ed Stetzer would state things differently. Now you would need at least a twelve-passenger van, if not a school bus. And I suspect in a few years, there won't be any elbow room in a small city. Over the last few decades, there has been a sea change of opinion on same-sex practice and gay marriage—not only in the culture but also in the church.

When I was an undergraduate at Wheaton College in the mid-1990s (before the invention of the iPhone or the regular use of email), students didn't talk about same-sex practice; it was simply off our radar. Who, then, would have thought that just over a decade later, a large group of

Wheaton students would assemble on the steps of Edman Chapel to protest as a well-known Christian author shared her story of how she came to Christ and renounced her lesbian past?[2] Or consider that as I was writing this chapter, I learned that one of Christianity's leading philosophers and public intellectuals, Nicholas Wolterstorff, had just come out in support of same-sex marriage—not only civil marriage, but ecclesial marriage. Back in October 2016, at an event in Grand Rapids, Michigan, Wolterstorff said, "When those with homosexual orientation act on their desires in a loving, committed relationship, [they] are not, as far as I can see, violating the love command."[3] During my undergraduate days as a philosophy major at Wheaton, Wolterstorff was one of my heroes. His books helped root me in my newfound faith and orient me to the life of the mind. This bit of news, then, was not only surprising but, if I'm honest, disappointing.

My wife, Katie, recently had a similar experience. Like many people across the country, she'd been challenged by popular Christian author Glennon Doyle Melton's *New York Times* bestselling book *Love Warrior*.[4] It's a gritty and insightful look at marriage, the life of recovery, and the path toward greater self-understanding. Melton's book has touched the lives of tens of thousands, even entering the inner sanctum of Oprah's Book Club, a coveted privilege for any writer interested in expanding their book's reach. Many were saddened when she announced in August 2016 that she was separating from her husband and the father of their three children. But the bombshell came three months later when she revealed to more than six hundred thousand Facebook followers that there was a new love in her life—female soccer star Abby Wambach. "Oh my God, she is so good to me. She loves me for all the things I've always wanted to be loved for. She's just my favorite. My person."[5]

These are a few cultural snapshots that hit close to home. If I were to cast a wider net, I would gather in many more. I share these simply to underscore the sea change of opinion on same-sex practice in our culture and in the church. What was unimaginable even a decade ago when President Bill Clinton signed into law the Defense of Marriage Act (DOMA) has now become the law of the land, when the United States Supreme Court recently ruled in *Obergefell v. Hodges* to legalize same-sex marriage in all fifty states—surely one of the most rapid and profound shifts of opinion in American history. But more remarkable still is the fact that evangelicals have kept pace with this sea change of opinion.

Ed, we're going to need more than an S.U.V.

## How Can a "God Boy" Think Gay Is Okay?

All of this forces us to pause and ask, "What has happened?" Why have there been such dramatic changes in the way evangelicals view same-sex practice and gay marriage?[6] How could something so obviously problematic to believers living just a generation ago become so widely embraced today, not least by Bible-carrying, conservative evangelicals? Or to put it more simply, as has been done effectively in a recent book, How can a "God Boy" come to think gay is okay?[7]

The reasons for this revolution in understanding are complex.[8] Significant intellectual and cultural trends have been at work under the surface of our society for decades, if not longer, like tectonic plates imperceptibly shifting until they collide and cause all of us to shake. At the risk of over-simplifying, let me suggest two factors that go a long way toward helping explain why evangelicals find it easy or even necessary to affirm same-sex practice or gay marriage.

First, evangelicals have experienced a profound loss of functional biblical authority. This rising generation of Christians has come of age in a world marked by "perva-sive interpretive pluralism"—a phrase coined by sociologist Christian Smith and forcefully presented in his book *The Bible Made Impossible.*[9] This is what it means: Your average evangelical Christian knows that the Bible can be used to support a number of different views on a host of important issues. Take any passage of Scripture, and you'll find sincere Christians who hold one view—and a similar number of equally devout believers who hold an opposing view.

What does pervasive interpretive pluralism look like in real life? Let me give you one example. Back in March 2014, popular Christian speaker, blogger, and author Jen Hatmaker took issue with Christian relief organization World Vision's decision that they would no longer refuse to hire people in same-sex marriages (a decision they later reversed). She took to her blog and wrote a critical response. I want to draw your attention to a few lines that reveal the presence of pervasive interpretive pluralism: "Thousands of churches and millions of Christ-followers faithfully read the Scriptures and with thoughtful and academic work come to different conclusions on homosexuality (and countless others). **Godly, respectable leaders have exegeted the Bible and there is absolutely not unanimity on its interpretation.** *There never has been.*"[10]

Neither Jen Hatmaker nor any other evangelical Christian would suggest that the Bible is a wax nose to be shaped however you choose. I don't know any Bible-loving believer who would make such a radical claim about Scripture. Jen Hatmaker surely wouldn't. But I do know plenty of Christians, perhaps you do as well, who have concluded that we can't reach a consensus on what the Bible really teaches. So they have resigned themselves to the idea that there isn't enough biblical material to make an open-and-shut case for much of anything—not least same-sex practice. And so, the reality of pervasive interpretive pluralism undercuts the functional authority of the Bible in the lives of these Christians. It's not that they dispense with the Bible; it's just that Scripture no longer speaks decisively on many issues, at least not on the issue of same-sex practice.

A second factor influencing the opinion of evangelicals on same-sex practice is the refashioning of moral intuitions. Our moral intuitions are those pre-theoretical responses we have to particular actions, those gut-level responses that tell us whether something is right or wrong before we even think about it.[11] In his book *The Righteous Mind*, moral psychologist Jonathan Haidt gives several examples of our moral intuitions at work. How do we know it's wrong to urinate on the American flag? Or why are we so confident it's not right to eat a dead pet for dinner rather than bury it in the backyard? Did we logically reason our way to these conclusions? No, probably not. In fact, we would have a hard time explaining exactly why either of these actions is wrong. We just know in our gut that they are.

Now for many in previous generations, same-sex intimacy struck them as odd, if not offensive, not because they reasoned their way to that conclusion, but because they felt it was wrong somewhere in their gut. They had a moral intuition, or an intuitive sense, that something was wrong with same-sex intimacy. It didn't need to be explained; it just was. (Sadly, this same moral intuition has been the driver behind an untold amount of harm done to gays and lesbians. When people see same-sex practice as gross or disgusting, they will have a hard time not acting in ways that are callous, bigoted, homophobic, and ultimately dehumanizing.) By contrast, for many in this present generation, displays of same-sex intimacy are not met with those same sorts of feelings. Not because they have reasoned their way to approving the moral status of same-sex practice, but because their moral intuitions have been fashioned (or refashioned) in a way that causes them to see same-sex intimacy as perfectly normal and unobjectionable.

How did this happen? No doubt the normalization of same-sex relationships in popular culture has done much to shape moral intuitions about same-sex intimacy. But the key factor is not the media, but relationships. Unlike their parents, most younger evangelicals know gays and lesbians as classmates and teammates, as colleagues and friends. Because of this, they see their lives and relationships, know their stories and struggles, and appreciate in many cases the dignity and sanctity of who they are as people—even in their same-sex relationships. Swiss theologian Karl Barth pointed this out years ago when he said that Christians need to reckon with the fact that many same-sex relationships are "redolent of sanctity."[12] In other words, they're hard to dismiss as sinful and wrong— regardless of what the Bible says or the church teaches.

What, then, has been the upshot of these two factors coming together in the hearts and minds of many evangelical Christians? To borrow a concept from the sociologists, it has undermined the "plausibility structure" of historic Christian sexual ethics.[13] For an increasing number of Christians, the Bible's teaching about human sexuality in general, and homosexuality in particular, no longer makes sense. At best, it seems quaint, like an antique that no longer serves any good purpose; at worst, it strikes many as offensive, like a pre–civil rights view of blacks as less than human. Either way, what centuries of Christians have always believed has nowadays become a point of stumbling, while same-sex relationships and other departures from historic Christian sexual ethics seem normal, even laudable.

## A Truncated Vision of Human Sexuality

Underlying both of these factors is an even more decisive issue—a truncated vision of human sexuality. We've lost sight of a positive Christian vision for why God made us as sexual beings in the first place. We've lost our grip on the deep logic that connects our created nature as male and female with how we ought to live relationally and sexually with one another. What used to be assumed by Christians of all denominational stripes has been lost in the confusion of our post-Christian culture. Listen to what *New York Times* columnist Ross Douthat says about the 1960s sexual revolution's impact on us: "Over the course of a decade or so, a large swath of America decided that two millennia of Christian teaching on marriage and sexuality were simply out of date."[14] We are suffering from a loss of vision.

Which is why the challenge we face is not one, but many. We confront dozens of challenges in matters of sexuality, each of which is an expression of this underlying loss of vision: alarmingly high rates of premarital sex, increasing cohabitation, adultery, divorce, out-of-wedlock births, dysfunctional sexual relations between spouses, the hook-up culture on college campuses, sexual abuse, and of course pornography. As biblical scholar Luke Timothy Johnson wryly points out, "There is more than enough sexual disorder among heterosexuals to fuel moral outrage."[15]

If we're going to live into the fullness of the gospel and

pursue sexual wholeness and holiness, we need to rediscover the Christian vision of human sexuality I call "mere sexuality."

So what is it? What is mere sexuality?

I'm using the word *sexuality* in a more general sense than we might normally use it. We tend to use the word to refer to a person's sexual activities, habits, or desires. In other words, sexuality almost always connotes sexual activity. But I'm using the word in a more general way to refer to the state or condition of being biologically sexed as either male or female. Philosophers will use the word *sexuate* to refer to the state or condition of being biologically sexed, and *sexuality* to refer to sexual activity or desire.[16] That's a nice terminological move, but since it is uncommon and sounds a bit unusual, I've chosen not to use the word *sexuate* in this book, even though it captures the way in which I will use the word *sexuality*.

On this understanding of the word *sexuality*, it would make sense to talk of a child's sexuality because that child is biologically sexed, even though he or she has not experienced sexual activity or sexual desire. It would also make sense to talk about Jesus' sexuality, even though Jesus never engaged in sexual activity and was free from illicit sexual desire.

But what about that little four-letter word *mere* in the phrase "mere sexuality"? You may be familiar with a famous book that has a similar-sounding title, C. S. Lewis's classic *Mere Christianity*. For Lewis, "mere Christianity" was a shorthand way to refer to the basic themes that have characterized the Christian faith through the ages. It's not Baptist Christianity or

Anglican Christianity or Presbyterian Christianity or Roman Catholic Christianity, but *mere* Christianity—the convictions all these streams share in common; in other words, what virtually all Christians everywhere have always believed.

By using the phrase "mere sexuality," I have something similar in mind. I use it as a shorthand way to refer to the themes that have characterized the Christian vision of sexuality down through the ages. By calling it "mere sexuality," I'm saying this is what most Christians at most times in most places have believed about human sexuality—in other words, the historic consensus.

Does such a consensus exist? Yes, there is a historic consensus about human sexuality that has been part of the church in each of its major expressions—Orthodox, Catholic, and Protestant. It has been around for centuries, from roughly the fourth to the middle of the twentieth century. And it has only seriously been called into question within the last forty to fifty years with the liberalization of Christian sexual ethics in the foment of the 1960s sexual revolution.

This does not mean there has been complete unanimity on every issue in the Christian tradition. For example, Gregory of Nyssa, the fourth-century Cappadocian father, believed that human beings would reproduce asexually in heaven, while Thomas Aquinas, the thirteenth-century Dominican priest, strongly disagreed. Yet Aquinas was of the opinion, following his esteemed philosophical master Aristotle, that women were "misbegotten males," a dubious view that subsequent Christian tradition rightly and roundly rejected. Augustine, bishop of Hippo and author of *Confessions* and *The City of God*, doubted whether sexual desire could ever rise above the level of lust. Martin Luther, however, begged to differ—as did John Calvin and others following in their Protestant wake. Or in his massive study of human sexuality, Pope John Paul II offers rather specific proposals about femininity and feminine values that, say, the famed Swiss theologian Karl Barth would have found deeply problematic on both methodological and christological grounds.

So there is real diversity and even divergence within the church's tradition, and we don't want to paper over those differences. Yet despite these disagreements, the consensus I'm calling "mere sexuality" has been surprisingly robust through the centuries, and we can identify its basic contours. They include a number of interrelated beliefs and convictions, but at the heart of mere sexuality, and of the church's historic teaching on human sexuality, is the belief that sexual difference, being male or female, is both theologically and morally significant. It matters to God, and it ought to matter to us.[17]

In the very first chapter of the Bible, we read that "male and female [God] created them" (Genesis 1:27). Immediately, then, we're confronted with both the canonical and theological priority of sexual difference in Christian thinking. It is essential to who we are, not accidental or peripheral, flexible or negotiable. Sexual difference is part of our nature as creatures. It is not something we create, like iPhones or automobiles. God has woven sexual difference into the fabric of creation. And because of this, our being male and female is integral to our calling as image bearers, not least in that most basic of all human communities—the one known as marriage. As a result, we can't ignore or minimize the fact of our being either male or female without undermining our ability to flourish and find fulfillment.

And since our sexual difference is core to who we are, it will not be eradicated at the resurrection but will persist for eternity, though in a fully glorified expression. Our resurrection bodies will be sexed bodies, just as Jesus' risen body is a sexed body. He is, and always will be, a crucified, circumcised Jewish male.

These, then, are the basic contours of what has been a time-honored and widespread Christian consensus on sexual difference, with implications that touch virtually every dimension of our lives. This is what I'm calling "mere sexuality"—what most Christians at most times in most places have believed about human sexuality.

## A More Robust Approach

By calling this vision "mere sexuality," I tap into what Christians of the past have consistently taught and what the vast majority of ordinary believers have always thought. In other words, I appeal to church tradition—and make no apologies for that. Mere sexuality is what celebrated philosopher Alasdair MacIntyre calls a living tradition—"an historically extended, socially embodied argument."[18] Christians' views on sexuality go back nearly two millennia and have been embodied in the lives of ordinary believers the world over. This is itself a strong, albeit not a decisive, argument in support of mere sexuality—and, incidentally, a strong word of caution to those who depart from it.[19] The problem is that this living tradition is now on life support as it drifts inexorably toward death, at least in the minds of many Christians. The church has forgotten what it has always believed.

In an age of rampant postmodern uncertainty, where sincere Christians disagree about a growing number of things they used to take for granted, it's important for evangelicals to retrieve this historic consensus. Many evangelicals have been weaned on a way of reading the Bible that is superficial and has proven itself largely unable to withstand the destabilizing effect of competing interpretations. Far too many strong Bible believers are committed to Scripture but skeptical of tradition. As a result, they operate with a bastardized view of the classic Protestant doctrine of Scripture—not *sola scriptura* ("Scripture alone"), but *nuda scriptura* ("Scripture in isolation"). But this emaciated approach can't stand its ground in the face of the twin challenges of pervasive interpretive pluralism and the widespread refashioning of moral intuitions.

This is why I'm convinced that redoubled efforts to lay out what the Bible really teaches about homosexuality, or about any other aspect of Christian sexual ethics for that matter, will take us only so far—or keep us tethered to orthopraxy for only so long. Serious engagement with what the Bible says on these matters is necessary, and I applaud these efforts. But they aren't sufficient in themselves to withstand the cultural and philosophical challenges we face. Such efforts may convert a choir member or two, but we'll be preaching to the choir. They will do little to give pause to those who have become disaffected with historic Christian sexual ethics.

My point is that our strategy needs to be more robust. It is time for evangelicals to rediscover the historic Christian vision of human sexuality. Now, more than at any time since the first centuries of the church, we need a countercultural Christian sexual ethic and, at an even deeper level, a distinctively Christian view of human sexuality. We need a fresh encounter with what has been called the "jarring gospel of Christian sexuality" that transformed the pagan world.[20] We need to recover the moral logic behind Christian sexuality: how babies relate to marriage, and marriage to sex, and sex to identity, and identity to being male and female—and how all of this relates to the person of Christ. That's where we're headed in this book. And we begin our journey in an unlikely place—with the sexuality of Jesus.

# CHAPTER 2

# THE SEXUALITY
# OF JESUS

I suspect that when you read the title of this chapter, you did a double take. The sexuality of Jesus? What does that mean? It may even strike you as oxymoronic, like calling Mother Teresa mean or Michael Jordan modest. The two don't go together.

If you're like most people, you've never heard a sermon on the sexuality of Jesus. Nor have you read a book on the subject. You know you've never taken a class, and you can't recall ever having read a blog that dealt with the sexuality of Jesus. You're not to blame. It's something Christians hardly ever think about. We seldom pause to reflect on the fact that Jesus is biologically sexed, just like you and me.

But therein lies the problem. Because we don't think about the sexuality of Jesus, we have to figure out what it means to be biologically sexed without any light from the One who reveals what it means to be truly human—Jesus Christ. We can't draw meaningful connections between who Jesus is as a biologically sexed person and who we are as biologically sexed persons. Or to put the problem theologically, we're left to cobble together a theological anthropology (of what it means to be a sexed human being) without the grounding of Christology, which is like explaining suffering apart from the sovereignty of God.[1]

Somewhere along the way, Christians divorced the Bible's teaching on human sexuality from the Bible's teaching on the humanity of Jesus. As a result, we turned the good news of God's intentions for human sexuality into a stale set of moral rules, a decidedly unevangelical thing to do. But this is what happens when we separate Christian ethics from the Christian gospel.[2] We're left with moralism, holding moral convictions without evangelical roots, and legalism, promoting Christian behavior by rules rather than by the gospel. But these two ugly curmudgeons will leech the life out of you and leave you with nothing but guilty feelings.

Mark Regnerus, an expert on the sex lives of American youth, has found that Christian teens have a decidedly unevangelical approach to sexual ethics; that is, they don't connect Christ to sex. "The majority of religious interviewees with whom we spoke . . . could articulate nothing more about what their faith has to say about sex than a simple no-sex-before-marriage rule. For most of them, this is the sum total of Christian teaching on sex."[3]

But what happens when Christians lose sight of Christ and look only to rules? Sadly, they become self-righteous and condescending. They cluck their tongues at those who drink, spit, and chew—or date girls who do. But that's not an appealing witness to those outside or inside the church. Americans are weary of the church's moralism and legalism. It all sounds so hypocritical, if not antihomosexual.[4] And the world tunes it out. But so too do many Christians, who are worn-out by aggressive rhetoric and insensitive behavior and ready to try something different, even if it means leaving the fold of the faithful, as young people are doing in droves.[5]

## The Missing Person in Sexuality Debates

If we're going to recover God's vision for human sexuality, then we need to rediscover the centrality of Christ for Christian sexual ethics. We need to reflect on how Jesus' humanity informs our understanding of human sexuality. But this won't be easy. There is little precedent for this sort of reflection. Jesus is glaringly absent from most discussions of human sexuality or homosexuality.

Don't misunderstand what I'm saying here. I've read dozens of books and articles on sexuality in general and homosexuality in particular, and many of them are quite good. And of course, many of them address, often insightfully, what Jesus thought or taught about sexuality or homosexuality. So I'm not saying there is a lack of reflection on the teaching of Jesus on human sexuality. Rather, what I'm saying is that there's a lack of reflection on the person of Jesus for human sexuality.

Take, for example, the debate over whether God solemnizes same-sex practice. In these discussions, people always appeal to what Jesus thought and taught. Those who support same-sex intimacy point to what Jesus said about love and inclusion, while those who oppose it emphasize what Jesus thought about marriage. And they debate this back and forth, round and round, seemingly with no end in sight. But I've noticed that in these discussions, no one pauses to ask a different question: not what Jesus thought or taught, but who Jesus was and is—and what significance it may have for our understanding of human sexuality or homosexuality.

In his book *People to Be Loved*, my friend Preston Sprinkle devotes a chapter to what Jesus thought and taught about homosexuality. He opens his discussion with an important question: "Where does Jesus stand on the question of homosexuality?" Preston rightly understands that "Jesus' words and actions should profoundly shape how we approach our topic."[6] And he does a good job of showing that Jesus' words and actions challenge both the affirming and nonaffirming crowds. It's a very well-written and well-taken chapter. But it left me wanting more—not more on what Jesus thought or taught, but more on who Jesus was and is, and on what Jesus' sexuality might mean for how we think about human sexuality and homosexuality. Or is there no moral or theological significance to the fact that Jesus was born of a virgin? Or that he lived a chaste and celibate life? Or that he never married? Or that his resurrection body is a male body? Are these facts only incidental to who Jesus is, not essential? Are they window dressing on his life, with cosmetic but not cosmic significance?

Christians have often struggled to take seriously the full humanity of Jesus, not least his being biologically sexed. Writes Debra Hirsh, "We have inadvertently cultivated a sexless Jesus."[7] The reasons for this are complex. But perhaps the leading culprit is an ancient heresy known as docetism, various forms of which still impact the thinking of Christians today. At root, this is the mistaken and unbiblical view that the earthly life of Jesus was a facade, not reality. The "real" Jesus is to be found in his divinity, not his humanity. And so docetism encourages Christians to discount the humanity of Jesus—it's illusory and insignificant. As is the case with many heresies in church history, a sincere desire to uphold the majesty of Christ leads inadvertently to the church losing contact with Jesus' actual humanity.[8]

This is what I sometimes call the "Clark Kent is really Superman" view of Jesus. Clark Kent, you'll remember, is the human guise for the otherworldly Man of Steel, born of an alien race from another planet, Krypton. Superman dons this human facade so he can mingle with the lowly humans, work at the *Daily Planet*, rescue a few of us from imminent danger, and fall in love with Lois Lane. But that's not who he really is—no, he's Superman. The thick, dark glasses; the JC Penney suit; the slicked-over hair—they're all just part of the guise. Behind the veneer is the real person. For the human being known as Clark Kent, it's Superman. For the earthly Jesus, it's the divine Son of God.

## God Chose a Y Chromosome

Christians for centuries have insisted that a close reading of the Bible teaches us something very different. Jesus didn't play the part of a human being. He was real flesh and blood. As some very earthy passages in Hebrews remind us, Jesus "partook of the same things" as us (2:14 ESV). He was "fully human in every way" (2:17). He even "suffered when he was tempted" (2:18).

Passages like these and others point to the mysterious Christian doctrine of the incarnation—the wondrous fact that God has become human in Christ. Jesus does not simply look like a man. He is a full-fledged human being like us—"with all the essential properties and common infirmities thereof, yet without sin" is the way the Westminster Confession of Faith nicely puts it.[9] Fully God and fully human at the same time—that's what the church has always taught.

But let's not stop there. Jesus became like us, not only in our humanity, but also in our sexuality—that is, his body is a biologically sexed body just like ours. The Word became flesh (John 1:14), but more than that, took on sexual difference, gender, hormones, and all the rest. God the Son became human, not in some abstract or general way, but in a very specific, embodied way—as a particular male human being. So what's true for you and me is also true for Jesus: "The whole of his existence was conditioned by his sexuality."[10]

Let me put it a bit more simply and bluntly: Through the incarnation, God the Son has a Y chromosome, facial hair, a higher basal metabolism rate—all the physiology, anatomy, and biochemistry that are distinctive to being a male. He didn't come as an intersex person whose condition eludes standard medical classification as male or female. Nor did he come as a sexless creature, like legions of angels who are neither male nor female. Instead, the Word of God took on a particular kind of human flesh—the kind that goes through puberty, grows armpit hair, has a ring finger longer than his index finger, a deeper voice than most women, and a penis.

Some of you might be wondering, *Where is he going with this?* Rest assured, we'll get there. And I want to clarify that I raise this point not to suggest in any way that men have an edge over women in relating to God. While some may try to make that argument, they would be wrong. Rather, I raise it to emphasize that the Son could have done either of the things I mentioned above, but he chose not to. He could have revealed the fullness of deity in lots of ways, but he chose to reaffirm the basic binary sexuality of creation by becoming a man.

What about the other half of the equation—woman? Does the incarnation speak to her? Yes, it does. By embracing human nature, God the Son embraced the Virgin's womb. The Second Person of the Trinity swam in amniotic fluid, fed from an umbilical cord, traveled a vaginal canal, and fed at his mother's breast. Pause to consider the significance of that. Or ponder these words: "Through the umbilical cord, he is this particular man, the son of this particular woman, the bearer of the whole previous genetic history of her people and the recipient of innumerable hereditary features."[11] The point is this: Through the incarnation, God the Son embraced male and female sexuality to the core. He didn't sidestep human sexuality; rather, he embraced it fully.

But we can say more. The incarnation shows us there is no male sexuality without female sexuality. We can't understand Jesus' sexuality without also grasping Mary's sexuality. Yes, the incarnation reveals the goodness of our being biologically sexed, but it also underscores the interdependence and complementarity of being male and female. Or as Paul aptly puts it, "In the Lord woman is not independent of man, nor is man independent of woman. For as woman came from man, so also man is born of woman" (1 Corinthians 11:11–12). This is true not only of us, but of God incarnate.

I'll go even one step further. Through the incarnation, the Son embraced the sexual differentiation that is core to mere sexuality. In fact, the incarnation testifies eloquently to the theological and moral significance of sexual difference— male and female. Sexual differentiation is not simply a feature of creation that God blesses and declares to be good; it is an essential part of our creaturely existence and one that the Son himself willingly embraced.

## The Resurrection Enshrines Mere Sexuality for Eternity

Yet the story of Jesus' sexuality doesn't end with the incarnation. We need to look further ahead in the story—to the resurrection. What do we learn about human sexuality from Jesus' resurrection? We see that the resurrection didn't bring an end to the Son's bodily existence or his male sexuality. When Jesus of Nazareth was raised from the dead, he didn't stop being human or cease being male.

We find continuity between Jesus' incarnation and his resurrection. Jesus is still Jesus—he's still as much a human being, and a man, as he ever was. Even now, in heaven, he has the same anatomy as he did before the resurrection. He exists, at this present moment, as a male human being, not a sexless apparition. So he could say to his disciples after his resurrection, "Look at my hands and my feet. It is I myself! Touch me and see; a ghost does not have flesh and bones, as you see I have" (Luke 24:39).

But we can say even more. The Second Person of the Trinity, the Son who took on flesh in the person of Jesus, will continue his embodied existence as a man for all eternity. Think about that for a moment. When the Son chose a Y chromosome and embraced human flesh, he did so forever—never to take it off or hang it up like an old worn-out coat. Our humanity, including our sexual difference, has become an intrinsic part of who God the Son is—and who God the Son will be forever.

Mere sexuality connects with Jesus Christ at two key points: in his incarnation and in his resurrection. In the incarnation, Jesus embraced sexual differentiation by taking on male flesh and traveling the Virgin's womb. And at the resurrection, when God raised Jesus bodily, he enshrined sexual difference for all eternity. God affirms his intentions in creation and promises that they will continue forever. Even when this old earth is no more, the new heavens and earth have dawned, and "people will neither marry nor be given in marriage; they will be like the angels in heaven" (Matthew 22:30). There will still be male and female. The risen Jesus is proof.

These two spectacular events—incarnation and resurrection—form the theological basis for mere sexuality. We see God's Yes! and Amen! to sexual differentiation. Male and female are not only part of the original creation but also part of the new creation. Our being biologically sexed is not only for this age but for the age to come as well.

## Celibacy and Sexual Fulfillment

But we're not done yet. These reflections on Jesus' incarnation and resurrection form the baseline for our thinking about human sexuality, but there's still a large chunk of his story we need to consider—his entire earthly life. What do we learn about our sexuality from Jesus' earthly life? One of the most important truths we should reflect on is this: No one was more fully human or sexually contented than Jesus, yet Jesus never engaged in a single sexual act. Think about it. Jesus never enjoyed the pleasures of sex, an erotic touch, or a lingering kiss. And he never indulged sexual fantasy or lust of the kind he roundly condemns, even though Scripture says that Jesus is "one who has been tempted in every way, just as we are" (Hebrews 4:15). And yet, as one biblical scholar has pointed out, "The Gospels portray a compelling and attractive person, who engages seriously with people and is good company at a party. Yet all the evidence is that he lived as a sexual celibate."[12]

Sadly, in our hypersexualized contemporary culture, it is almost inconceivable that someone could be sexually chaste, even celibate, and experience the fullness of what it means to be human and the peace of sexual contentment. Our culture is such that sexual activity is viewed as the most direct path to personal fulfillment and self-realization—to being truly human and fully alive. So deep-seated is this belief that most people today think that to deny yourself sexual experiences is to undermine your own humanity. Try floating the idea of sexual chastity to a group of college freshmen or young urban professionals, and see what kind of looks you get.

But Jesus' life deconstructs this pervasive and powerful cultural myth. His life says something different. From the story of his life, we learn that sexual activity isn't essential to human flourishing or personal fulfillment. Jesus found contentment with his sexuality in the pursuit of chastity and celibacy. To be blunt, he didn't need sex—not because sex is sinful or somehow beneath his dignity, but because sex isn't essential to being human.

The Son of God, though biologically sexed, lived a sex-free, fully contented life. Not an easy, pain-free existence, but a whole and deeply and richly human life. This is a remarkable fact—one that confronts all of us, whether we're same-sex-attracted or straight, married or single. It also confronts our secular culture and the evangelical church culture as well—I suspect in some uncomfortable ways. Frankly, as a happily married heterosexual, I find it's easy to forget (and tempting to resist the idea) that I don't need sex to be satisfied. Jesus didn't, and yet he was supremely satisfied in God. That humbles me, much like the prospect of fasting from food humbles me.

One of the main claims of mere sexuality, as it has been articulated and practiced throughout the church's history, is that while sexuality (our being biologically sexed as male and female) is central to what it means to be human, sexual activity is not. If we want to be fully human, we have to embrace our sexed bodies. But we don't have to engage in sexual activity to be fully human. The life of the Son of God makes that perfectly clear.

Our culture has this backward though. It says that our biological sex, whether we're male or female, is secondary. This is why bisexualism and transgenderism are on the rise. This is also why, as we enter a "post-gay" world, people will view their biologically sexed body, not as a graciously given and fixed feature of their identity, but as an option to consider and, if need be, renegotiate to better align with their sense of self or suit their goals and ambitions. Caitlyn Jenner is a famous case in point. As she affirms on her blog, "I'm learning every day what it means to live as my true self."[13]

On the other hand, our culture insists, ironically enough, that sexual activity is essential to human fulfillment—that you can't be human without it. If you've ever seen a Cialis or Viagra commercial, you understand the gut-level appeal of this way of thinking. But here's where our culture is confusing. We're told that our biological sex is optional—whether you're male or female, or whether you're attracted to male or female, doesn't much matter. In the words of pop icon Miley Cyrus, "I don't relate to being boy or girl, and I don't have to have my partner relate to boy or girl."[14] Yet we're also told that engaging in sexual activity is essential. No sex, no life. Sex, life.

But as we've seen, the life of Jesus tells a different story. I like the way the renowned New Testament scholar and ethicist Richard Hays summarizes the challenging truth Jesus brings to our sex-crazed culture: "Despite the smooth illusions perpetrated by mass culture in the United States, sexual gratification is not a sacred right, and celibacy is not a fate worse than death."[15]

## Torn by the Prospect of Lifelong Celibacy

In preparation for writing this book, I read many books and articles on the theme of human sexuality—and homosexuality in particular. Several were autobiographical in nature and helped me better understand the experience of those who are same-sex-attracted. One of the most compelling narratives I read was Justin Lee's in his book *Torn: Rescuing the Gospel from the Gays-vs.-Christians Debate.*

Justin grew up in a strong Bible-believing home and identifies as an evangelical Christian. But Justin also identifies as gay. In his book, he talks movingly about when he first realized he was gay and began wrestling with what that meant. How could he be faithful to Scripture yet live with consistent same-sex attraction? For Justin there's no easy answer. He recognizes that the Christian church has held the view for centuries that God doesn't sanction same-sex sexual intimacy. Yet he's daunted by the prospect of lifelong celibacy:

> No relationship, no sex, no romance. I didn't like the sound of that at all. Still, I knew that if I wanted to serve Christ with my life, and if He was calling me to celibacy, then I would have to be celibate.
>
> [Yet] I considered what this would mean. Obviously, it would mean no sex. Ever.
>
> Imagine telling any teenage boy that he can never have sex, that he must go his entire life without being able to experience it even once. I imagine his response would be less than enthusiastic. Mine was likewise. As a teenager, abstaining from sex is difficult enough

when you know you're waiting for the right time. It's far more difficult when you know there will never be a right time, even if you find the right person.[16]

Justin goes on to confess that his real struggle with celibacy is not forgoing sex, but letting go of the possibility of deep intimacy and companionship:

> It wasn't just the physical pleasure I wanted; I craved the intimacy of sex. I craved the experience of total vulnerability with another human being . . .
>
> To go without sex was one thing, but to go without romance and companionship was quite another. People don't marry for the right to have sex; they marry for love and the opportunity to build a life together with another human being.[17]

If you're same-sex-attracted, then no doubt this humble and transparent confession resonates with you. But if you're not same-sex-attracted, then I encourage you to pay close attention to what Justin has written. Let it sink in, lay hold of you, work on your imagination, and stir up empathy. I don't think heterosexual Christians will begin to understand, much less love, our brothers and sisters in Christ who identify as gay or lesbian until we can sincerely empathize with this painful dilemma. Justin says he's torn by the prospect of lifelong celibacy, and we should be torn up for him. It's an unenviable situation without easy answers.

## Jesus Suffered When Tempted

At the same time, I should say that I have some deep disagreements with where Justin feels led in his personal pilgrimage. By the end of the book, he has come to the place where he affirms same-sex sexual activity, at least in certain situations. This is a momentous conclusion, yet I don't doubt his sincerity in coming to it. I do disagree, however, with the reasons he comes to this conclusion.

First, I part company with Justin on his interpretation of the key passages in Scripture that speak about same-sex practice. I won't delve into the specifics here. That's not the goal of this book, and others have more than adequately covered that ground.[18] But you should know that Justin's interpretations deviate from historic Christian understandings, as well as from mainstream evangelical scholarship.

Second, I don't think Justin has come to terms with mere sexuality. The church's stance against homosexual activity isn't the product of a few Bible proof texts that speak directly to the issue of same-sex practice; it is the result of the Bible's holistic vision of human sexuality, which pervades Scripture.

Third, I fear that Justin hasn't grappled seriously with the sexuality of our Savior—not just what Jesus thought or taught, but who he was and is. Let me elaborate on this third point.

Jesus was a lifelong celibate. The Son of God never had sex. He never enjoyed the thrill of romance. He never knew the rush or comfort of intimate sexual touch, nor did he experience the intimate caress of another human being. He never had the opportunity to build a life together in marriage with someone. He never knew what it was like to enjoy life-long marital companionship in that way. He was chaste, and he was celibate.

And may I add that this probably wasn't easy for Jesus, as though the celibate life was straightforward for the Son of God. We might get the impression that Jesus just cruised through life effortlessly, with zero struggle over the things with which you and I and Justin Lee struggle. But that's just not true. As the author of Hebrews writes, Jesus is not "unable to empathize with our weaknesses, but [is] one who has been tempted in every way, just as we are—yet he did not sin" (4:15). Or notice the profound phrase from a passage I quoted earlier—that "he himself suffered when he was tempted" (2:18).

To put it simply, Jesus gets it. He knows. He understands. He struggled with normal human life in a fallen world, yet was without sin. And we can also say that he struggled more profoundly than you or I ever could, because he never gave in to temptation. We often think that those who resist temptation do not know the struggle against sin, but this is entirely backward. C. S. Lewis rightly said, "Only those who try to resist temptation know how strong it is . . . Christ, because He was the only man who never yielded to temptation, is also the only man who knows to the full what temptation means—the only complete realist."[19] Those who give in to their sinful desires never truly understand the struggle of the one who resists. Jesus never yielded to temptation. He is the only complete realist, even in the area of human sexuality.

## Resurrection Brings Sexual Resolution

Earlier in this book, I referred to my friend Wesley Hill, who, like Justin Lee, is a committed evangelical believer who lives with consistent same-sex attraction. Wesley, like Justin, has wrestled with his sexuality and what it means for his life: the prospect of lifelong celibacy, no sex, no marriage. But Wesley has come to a different conclusion, and he has chosen a different path.

It's a path more in keeping with the vision of mere sexuality, with the church's historic position on the question of same-sex practice. And I believe it's a more difficult path than the one Justin Lee is now walking. I say that not to be disrespectful, but to honor the fact that Wesley is walking the road Jesus walked—the path of lifelong celibacy—in order to follow the teaching of the Bible and the example of Jesus. Wesley writes candidly about the suffering of temptation he experiences as one who is same-sex-attracted yet also striving in fidelity to Christ to live a life of sexual chastity, as Jesus did. Why, Wesley asks, would I as a same-sex-attracted person not go to bed with a partner of the same sex? Why wouldn't I seek the intimacy and enjoyment of sex with someone I find attractive?

In the end, what keeps me on the path I've chosen is not so much individual proof texts from Scripture or the sheer weight of the church's traditional teaching against gay sex. Instead, it is, I think, those texts and traditions and teachings *as I see them from within the true story of what God has done in Jesus Christ*—and the whole perspective on life and the world that flows from that story, as expressed definitively in Scripture.[20]

The key for Wesley is the sexuality of Jesus. Jesus' example holds him fast.

But this isn't a simple decision or an easy road for him: "We groan in frustration because of our fidelity to the gospel's call. And though we may miss out in the short run on lives of personal fulfillment and sexual satisfaction, in the long run the cruelest thing that God could do would be to leave us alone with our desires, to spare us the affliction of his refining care."[21]

Wesley goes on to describe the encouragement he has found in learning about the personal struggles of Henri Nouwen, who, like Wesley, was celibate and same-sex-attracted. He talks movingly about the "desire for love, affection, companionship, permanent intimacy, life-giving community, a deep sense of belonging, a safe haven, a home"—and the struggle to find these as a same-sex-attracted believer.[22]

Yet Wesley knows the only true resolution will be in his bodily resurrection. When God raised Jesus from the dead, he pointed us to the resolution of our own brokenness, sexual or otherwise. Wesley writes:

> Nearly two thousand years ago, Good Friday gave way to Easter Sunday, and at the end of history, when Jesus appears, death will give way to resurrection on a cosmic scale and the old creation will be freed from its bondage to decay as the new is ushered in. On that day, there will be no more loneliness. The wounds will be healed. I expect to stand with Henri Nouwen at the resurrection and marvel that neither of us is gay anymore, that we both—together with every other gay Christian—are whole and complete in the fellowship of the redeemed, finally at home with the Father.[23]

The resurrection of Jesus serves as a constant reminder that there is more to come. We are in bondage to sin and await the resurrection of the body. We will always struggle, in one way or another, more or less, all the time. There will always be parts of our lives that aren't fully resolved, whether we are homosexual or heterosexual, single or married—desires unfulfilled, hopes unmet, sins stubborn and unshakable. But the resurrection of Jesus reminds us that this universal human experience will one day come to an end. The resurrection is the resolution to all that troubles us, even our sexual experience. Resurrection brings sexual resolution.

The appeal of mere sexuality, then, goes beyond a handful of scriptural passages that explicitly address same-sex practice. It invites us to look to Jesus Christ himself, not in an abstract sense as the teacher of love or as the teacher of morality, but as the one who took on human flesh and lived a sexually fulfilled, sexually chaste, sacrificial life—all for the sake of others.

# CHAPTER 3

# MALE, FEMALE, AND THE *IMAGO DEI*

Recently I was driving my sixteen-year-old son Ezra to an activity at our church when, out of nowhere, he asked me, "Dad, why do people think gender is socially constructed?" I should tell you that Ezra is a bright and inquisitive kid, so this sort of question wasn't entirely unusual for him. But hearing him drop it in the middle of our ride to church did put a smile on my face. Still, I wanted to meet his seriousness with seriousness, so I readied a serious answer.

"Because gender *is* socially constructed," I said. "But sex isn't."

Ezra pondered that for a minute. "What's the difference?" he wondered aloud.

"Gender," I explained, "is how we live out our biological sex. It's how we act in light of whether we're male or female. And that tends to be different from culture to culture—at least a little bit different. What is feminine or masculine in our culture may not be the same in another culture. But sex, whether you're male or female, that's obviously not socially constructed, but a given, a part of nature. You either have a Y chromosome or you don't.

"The challenge, though," I continued, "is that many in our culture equate the two—sex and gender. And since gender is socially constructed, they mistakenly think that sex is too. Which is why, Ezra, you see lots of people treating both their gender and their biological sex as though they were inconsequential rather than as fundamental to who they are."

Ezra seemed content with this answer. Fortunately so, because we were pulling into the church parking lot. I stopped the car in front of the main entrance. Ezra hopped out, and we've not revisited the conversation since.

But similar conversations take place every day, all around us. Recently a member of our church was at the mall and overheard a brief conversation between a male vendor and a female customer. I share their exchange because it gives a good glimpse into how confused our culture is about the relationship between identity and sexuality:

**Customer:** "I just moved to Chicago from Portland. Things are pretty good in Portland. But before Portland, I lived in the South."

**Vendor:** "Oh, in the South their ideas of gender are so rigid!"

**Customer:** "I know. It was terrific when I got to Portland. It's all so amorphous. I tend to be

a tomboy anyway, and I just loved it there.
Everything is so free and undefined."

This is just one simple cultural snapshot, but it captures the way an increasing number of people view their sexuality in relation to their identity. They see their gender, and even their biological sex, as inconsequential to who they are. Being male or female, having facial hair or mammary glands, no more determines your identity than whether you wear a watch on your right or left wrist. It's a lifestyle choice. The argument is that whether you're anatomically male or female doesn't matter all that much for your identity. These biological features, and how we express them, aren't fixed; they're negotiable. We can choose our sexual identity—or so we're told.

We find evidence of this mind-set everywhere. Maybe you heard the news that a major retailer, Target, has decided to transition away from using gender-based signs in some of their departments. Why would they do this? Their marketing executives explain that these signs are too stereotyped for children, and that makes them bad for business. The cap guns are now next to the Barbie dolls.

Or perhaps you noticed back in February 2014 that Facebook added a new feature to your personal profile. You can now "customize" your gender, allowing you to choose from one of more than fifty alternatives. There still remains that old-fashioned binary of "male" and "female," but now there is also "transgender," "cisgender," "gender fluid," "intersex," "neither," and many, many more. The Facebook Help page explains what all of this means and the options you have: "If you set your gender to Custom and select one or more genders, you can also select an audience for your custom gender. In addition to your custom gender, you'll choose a Preferred Pronoun. The preferred pronoun you select is public."[1]

When Facebook announced their decision to the public, they explained the change this way:

> When you come to Facebook to connect with the people, causes, and organizations you care about, we want you to feel comfortable being your true, authentic self. An important part of this is the expression of gender, especially when it extends beyond the definitions of just "male" or "female." So today, we're proud to offer a new custom gender option to help you better express your own identity on Facebook.[2]

Did you notice the rationale here? Since our identity is something we determine, it must necessarily include our sexuality. The categories of male and female are too limiting. We need more options! After all, what right do our bodies have to tell us who we should be?

Consider another example, this time from Europe. You may have caught wind back in November 2013 that Germany became the first European country to allow a person to put on their child's birth certificate an "X" rather than either an "M" or "F" gender identification. I was intrigued to hear the BBC's take on this change. They interviewed a therapist named Sarah Graham, who celebrated this as a landmark step forward, a sign of progress in legislation: "This pink and blue thing is a nonsense. It's a hegemony that we need to challenge. We all need to be free. The human heart is the most important organ, not what goes on down there."[3]

In the United States and throughout the Western world, people increasingly view their biological sex and their gender as inconsequential rather than fundamental to who they are. At times this line of thinking is taken further, so that being born male or female is seen as a hindrance rather than a help in discovering your true identity. These are unprecedented developments propelling our culture into uncharted waters.

## You Are Who You Desire?

While our culture cuts the link between our sexuality and our identity, it also sends a clear message that our sexual desires determine our identity. The message we hear is that you are who you desire sexually—an unprecedented inflation of one aspect of our sexuality. We now live in a world of "sexual identities," and this is something quite new in the history of civilization. Jenell Williams Paris, a professor of anthropology at Messiah College, says in her fascinating book *The End of Sexual Identity*, "Of all humans who have ever lived, very few have had sexual identities."[4] She explains:

> Sexual identity is a Western, nineteenth-century for-
> mulation of what it means to be human. It's grounded
> in a belief that the direction of one's sexual desire is

identity-constituting, earning each individual a label (gay, lesbian, straight, etc.) and social role. Perceived as innate and as stemming from inner desire, sexual identity has to be searched out, found, named and expressed in order for each person to be a fully functional and happy adult. Finding our sexual feelings is part of how we come to know ourselves and present ourselves to others.[5]

This sexual identity framework now dominates the way we Westerners think about our sexuality and our identity; it has made one particular aspect of our sexuality, namely, our sexual desires and attractions, all-important in determining who we are.[6] The result is that in the late-modern world, there are now only two types of people—gays and straights. And even this is quickly becoming an antiquated way of thinking. There are now multiple variations on this basic distinction, depending on one's desires and attractions.

What does this mean for us practically? How does it affect the way we live? Consider this: if your teenage daughter were to notice that she has a strong affinity for those of the same sex, or even a degree of physical attraction, our culture would encourage her not simply to acknowledge these desires but to define herself on the basis of them. What does this sound like? Coming from a fourteen-year-old daughter, who by the way still isn't old enough to drive a car, vote, or drink a glass of wine, it sounds like this: "Mom and Dad, I'm a lesbian. That's just me; that's just who I am."

We live in a very confused and confusing culture when it comes to sexuality and identity. We hear mixed messages all the time. On the one hand, we hear that sexuality is everything, at least our sexual desires are. They determine who we are. On the other hand, we hear that sexuality is nothing, at least whether we're male or female. Our biological sex doesn't have much to do with who we are. In fact, our biological sex may be hindering us from fully expressing who we are.

Consider the story of Avery Wallace. He was born biologically a girl. But he says that since the age of two, he knew he was a boy. "I was 100 percent sure of who I was and biology was an insignificant part of the conversation." In an opinion piece he wrote for CNN when he was just fifteen, Avery explains: "I was a little boy expressing myself based on what was in my heart and mind—not yet distorted by biology, other people's confusion, or fear."[7] This is a remarkable statement. It reflects the triumph of the subjective over the objective, the victory of intuitions over bodies. Additionally, it reflects the full flowering of what theologian Oliver O'Donovan calls "psychological positivism," the mischievous idea that our inner desires are self-interpreting or at least easy to interpret.[8]

It's little wonder that we are, as a culture, quite an anxious bunch of folks. The times in which we live have scrambled the most basic and enduring categories we have for understanding who we are. In just a few decades, the long-standing norms that have always guided our understanding of personal identity and sexuality have changed. More accurately, they've disappeared. And we're left reeling as a result, not sure how to do life anymore. In fact, we're not even sure what it means to be human—to be male or female.

## "Male and Female He Created Them"

As is so often the case, the Bible clarifies what our culture confuses. The Bible says having sexed bodies is *essential* to our identity, not optional. It's a gift we receive, not a choice we make. Or as Rosaria Butterfield writes, "Bible-believing Christians are gender and sexuality *essentialists*."[9] But the Bible also says that our identity isn't reducible to one aspect of our sexuality, not even to our sexual desires or attractions.

Contrast this with our culture's messaging, which tells us that we are who we desire sexually—turning sexual desire into an idol that has power to name us in a way that should be left to God. The Bible connects our identity to what is called the *imago Dei*, or the image of God.[10] We find this expression in Genesis 1:26–27:

> Then God said, "Let us make mankind in our image, in our likeness, so that they may rule over the fish in the sea and the birds in the sky, over the livestock and all the wild animals, and over all the creatures that move along the ground."
>
> So God created mankind in his own image,
>     in the image of God he created them;
>     male and female he created them."

This is the first chapter of the Bible, and it is foundational to all the rest—not least our understanding of God and ourselves. On the sixth day, God creates human beings, his culminating act of creation. In verse 26, God speaks in the first person, as though he's more heavily invested in the creation of humans than, say, grasshoppers or walruses or even supernovas. Then in the next verse, God's clearly stated intention is given: "Male and female he created them." This statement is grammatically parallel with being created in the image of God in the first two parts of the verse. What is the significance of this? It means that being male and female is essential to being created in God's own image.

Reflect for a moment on the radical implications of this idea. When God creates a creature in his own image, after his likeness, he doesn't create a solitary individual, a genderless monad. Instead he creates a complementary pair—male and female. Not one, but two—and not two of the same, even though they are a lot alike.

That's what we are as male and female. We see these complementary similarities and differences hardwired into our bodies, even our anatomy. All of us come into this world with a vital part of who we are, whether male or female, specifically designed to complement another human being who is like us, yet different from us.

This is not all it means to be created in God's image—not by far—but it is one significant part of it. We are made in the image and likeness of a triune God. We were created as beings-in-relationship, as persons-in-community, just as God is Father, Son, and Holy Spirit. As one of the twentieth century's great theologians put it, "God is in relationship, and so too is the man created by him. This is his divine likeness."[11]

## Male or Female: Fidelity to Your Sexuality

Let's probe a bit further into what it means that God created us male and female. But before we do that, we should take a small step back and consider something even more basic. Each of us is created either male or female.[12] This may seem so obvious that it's not worth stating, but given the challenges we face, it does need to be pointed out. It's the clearest thing we can say about being created in the image of God. All of us are either one or the other. The tragic developmental anomaly of intersex notwithstanding, there really is no third option; there is just this basic dual reality.

When God created you in his image as male or female, he called you to a certain way of life—as either a male or a female. By virtue of being created in the image of God as male or female, you have a call on your life; you have a vocation. It is your most basic vocation, your most fundamental job in life: to joyfully embrace and faithfully embody your sexuality—whether male or female—for the good of others.[13]

God's first call on our lives is to acknowledge rather than deny our sexuality. We are to rejoice in it rather than seek to downplay it. We are to lean into it fully rather than avoid it entirely. We are to use our sexuality to bless others rather than neglect it to the loss of others. And we are to embrace its limits rather than try to transcend it.

There is always the temptation to depart from God's call on our lives as either male or female, to downplay or even deviate from who God has made us to be. Tragic things happen when we begin to despise our own sexuality and the bodies God has given us. When we fail to thank God for who he has made us to be and allow ingratitude to define our attitude toward God, the results can be very serious and sad. This is what Paul describes in Romans 1:21, where both men and women find their lives going off the rails in sexual ways, precisely because they failed to honor God or give him thanks.

Melinda Selmys, in her book *Sexual Authenticity*, describes how for years she wrestled with her own sexuality. She was a professed, practicing lesbian who underwent a profound transformation and eventually got married to a man. She explains how significant change came when she began to come to terms with her own sexuality and with who God had made her to be as a woman:

> I realized that my own sex was not inferior, that its strengths throughout the ages had always been strengths, that its contributions to the world were not second-class or insignificant. It was here, in this, that the cracks opened enough that I could risk falling in love with a man. Suddenly, I was not an interloper on his territory, trying to seize his castles and make them my own.

I had my own kingdom, my own square of land, my own integrity. I did not need to demand power: I had it. I did not need to take something of value away from him and hold it to ransom: I had valuable things of my own. At last, I understood something of who I was. Not lesbian. Not bisexual. Not gay. Not straight, either. But a woman, made in the image and likeness of God. In possession of myself, with the right and the ability to give the gift of myself to another, sincerely, in love.[14]

To be created in the image of God as male and female means that each of us is either male or female. We are called to embrace who God has made us to be, whether male or female. We must be faithful to our calling as male or female and must own who we are sexually as one of God's greatest gifts to us—for the good of others.

## Male and Female: Complementarity in our Sexuality

The truth that God has made us male and female is very good news. God not only created two genders, male and female, with unique and glorious and mysterious differences; he made these two genders complementary. They don't simply fit side by side, like peanut butter and jelly; they fit together in an interlocking pattern like puzzle pieces. They have been created for each other, to complete each other in the most profound sorts of ways. This means that to be faithful to your own sexuality, whether male or female, you can't idolize your own sex—as though your sex is the be-all and end-all of the human race. Sure, there's a place for donning the "Girls Rule" T-shirt or descending into the "man cave." Yes, there's a place for same-sex friendships and even a little "bromance." But the relationships we have with those of our own sex should not replace or exclude the beautiful dynamic at work when we relate to those of the opposite sex.

We need opposite-sex relationships not only to complement and strengthen the other sex but to learn more about our own sex. Women learn who they are as women by interacting with other women but also with men. So, too, men learn who they are by interacting not only with other men but with women as well. Interaction with the opposite sex is essential to our growth and self-understanding as creatures made in God's image as male and female. Karl Barth put it brilliantly: "It is always in relation to their opposite that man and woman are what they are in themselves."[15]

Think about what this means practically. You won't grow into the kind of person God wants you to become if you don't have meaningful relationships with those of the opposite sex. You can't, because the opposite sex isn't just some strange creature from another planet, but it is God's gift to you, as your complement, whether you are male or female.[16]

Of course, one of the most obvious ways this interaction between the two sexes takes place is in marriage. But that's not the only place we interact meaningfully (even if not sexually) with the opposite gender. If you are a man, you interact with the opposite sex all the time—mothers, sisters, friends, employers or employees, teachers, coaches, classmates, neighbors, aunts, cousins. So too, if you are a woman, you encounter men all the time—fathers, brothers, friends, employers or employees, teachers, coaches, classmates, neighbors, uncles, cousins.

Don't overlook these opportunities to learn about what it means to be who God has called you to be, whether male or female. We should grow to appreciate the distinctive yet complementary strengths males and females bring to every task, whether planning a party, running a business, cheering from the sidelines of a soccer game, or raising a family. We should not only appreciate but be dazzled by these complementary differences. Here is a beautiful description of the complementary gifts men and women bring to the parenting task as mothers and fathers:

> A wise father teaches his wife and family that in order to love you must be strong; a wise mother teaches her husband and family that in order to be strong you must love. She knows that even boldness needs humility; he knows that even humility needs to be bold. He is an animate symbol to his children of that justice which is tempered by mercy, she a living emblem of that mercy which is tempered by justice. Each of them refracts a different hue from the glowing light of royalty. A

wise father knows when to say, "ask your mother," a wise mother when to say, "ask your father." When they do this, they are not passing the buck, but sharing sovereignty.[17]

Male and female God created each of us. And this isn't something to despise or downplay, but to treasure and delight in. It's one of God's glorious gifts to us. We live in a culture that is confused and confusing, where sexuality and identity are put together in conflicting and even extreme ways. As Christians, however, we need to resist, on the one hand, the temptation to make too little of our sexuality, as though being created male and female doesn't much matter. On the other hand, we need to resist the equal and opposite temptation to make too much of our sexuality for our identity, treating sexual desires or attractions as determinative of who we are rather than letting God's Word define who we are.

Despite the consistent messaging of our culture, you are not who you desire sexually. Instead you are who God has created you to be in his image and likeness, whether male or female. And more importantly, you are who God calls you to be in his Son, Jesus Christ. Despite all our brokenness, despite all our failing to be fully and faithfully who we are as male or female, Jesus Christ welcomes us to find our identity ultimately in him.

# CHAPTER 4

# "ONE FLESH"

Marriage is a hotly contested issue in our culture today. For more than a decade, Americans have been engaged in a culture war over who should legally marry. The issue was "resolved" in June 2015 when the U.S. Supreme Court legalized same-sex marriage in all fifty states. But I suspect our country will debate this issue for years to come, much like another controversial judicial decision, Roe v. Wade.[1]

From this controversy, you might conclude that we're confused about what marriage is. And you might further think that if everyone could agree on a definition of marriage, then these cultural tensions would go away. I can appreciate that way of thinking because I thought similarly for years. But I've come to a very different conclusion. I'm now convinced that our problem isn't that we're confused about the definition of marriage; our problem is the opposite. Most Americans agree about what marriage is; it's just that our understanding of marriage is a serious misunderstanding. Let me explain what I mean.

Nowadays, many Christians and non-Christians share the same view of marriage. *But how can that be*, you ask, *when there is such disagreement between Christians and non-Christians over who is allowed legally to marry?* Even though they disagree about who can get married, they agree on what marriage is. Over the last fifty years, a new understanding of marriage has become normative in American society. It's a view now shared by the majority of people in our culture, whether inside or outside the church, whether people of faith or not.

It's what you might call a "companionate" view of marriage.[2] On this understanding, marriage is primarily about companionship—a deep, intimate, lasting relationship with another person. We see evidence of this view of marriage in popular culture and the media. But we also see it reflected in many Christian books and sermons on marriage. It is the view of marriage we observe when the maid of honor toasts the bride and groom by saying they've found their "soul mate," or the bride and groom say they have married their "best friend."[3] These gestures, and many others besides, reflect a companionate understanding of marriage. My guess is that you have heard this view of marriage expressed many times. You may even hold it yourself.

On this view, marriage is an enduring commitment you make to another person because of an intense emotional connection you have with that person. This view is also sometimes called the "romantic" view of marriage. A happy marriage is one based on intense feelings of attraction toward another person. It is rooted in a sense that marriage fulfills our emotional and relational needs in a unique way that will last in intensity and power for a lifetime. It is the dominant view of marriage within our culture among Christians and non-Christians alike.

## "They Shall Become One Flesh": Marriage as Comprehensive Union

What we find in the Bible is a different view of marriage. While elements of the companionate view are included in the biblical teaching, overall the Bible has a richer, fuller, more robust understanding of marriage. It's not any less intense or emotional. But it's a whole lot more than our emotions. This classic and historic Christian view of marriage has been the dominant view of marriage in Western culture—until relatively recently.

We find this view of marriage in the opening pages of the Bible where we read these words: "That is why a man leaves his father and mother and is united to his wife, and they become one flesh" (Genesis 2:24). Notice the phrase "one flesh." According to the biblical and historic Christian view, marriage is a one-flesh union. It's not just an emotional bond or a relational connection you feel with someone. Rather, it's a specific kind of union—a one-flesh union. It is a union of heart, mind, spirit, and body.[4] I like the way author Kevin DeYoung puts it: "The *ish* [man] and the *ishah* [woman] can become one flesh because theirs is not just a sexual union but a *reunion*, the bringing together of two differentiated beings, with one made *from* and both made *for* the other."[5]

There are many different ways we come together to join our lives in a common purpose. We create bowling leagues, soccer teams, academic societies, and labor unions, all of which unite people for a common purpose. But a marital union is a unique kind of union. It is a comprehensive union in which people join together not only mentally, emotionally, and spiritually but bodily as well.

That's why Scripture refers to marriage as a "one-flesh" union, not a one-heart or one-spirit or one-soul union. The uniting of bodies, of flesh, is essential, not optional. The language of "one flesh" is meant to be a very specific, concrete reference to your flesh, your physical body. But, frankly, we should be even more specific. The one-flesh union here is not just a uniting of bodies in some general way, like exchanging hugs or holding hands. It refers to a coming together of two bodies in a very specific way. The old-fashioned term for this coming together is *coitus*, the less old-fashioned term is *intercourse*, and today we just call it *sex*. It's what church tradition and common law have for centuries seen as the consummation of the marriage. Men and women have one, and only one, bodily organ that has been specifically designed for a complement, and when these two organs—the male and female sexual organs—come together to perform one unified and unifying act, they form a one-flesh union quite literally, physically, indeed even biologically.

Think about it this way. I have, as you no doubt do as well, strong emotional connections with lots of different people—my children, my parents, my sibling, my extended family, my fellow pastors, my close friends, and many in my church family with whom I'm united as brothers and sisters in Christ.

And yet I have a comprehensive union with none of these other people, but only with my wife. Only with her do I share and unite mentally, emotionally, spiritually, and—this is the key—bodily. This is a one-flesh union, a complete and total uniting of lives, and we have for centuries called this comprehensive union "marriage."

## Exclusivity: Leaving All Other Attachments

I don't think I can overemphasize how important this idea of a one-flesh union is for mere sexuality or for a Christian understanding of marriage. It is a game changer on almost every level, not just for how you view marriage but also for how you view virtually every other aspect of Christian sexual ethics. In fact, almost everything Christianity teaches about sexuality flows from this idea of marriage as a one-flesh union.

So let me linger here on this idea and explore two aspects of Christian sexual ethics that flow organically from this view of marriage as a one-flesh union. These two characteristics are directly tied to marriage as a comprehensive union that includes bodies.[6] The first characteristic is *exclusivity*. We find this feature embedded in Genesis 2:24: "That is why a man leaves his father and mother . . ." This is the language of the traditional wedding vows, where we "forsake all others and keep ourselves unto this one only," forming an exclusive covenant relationship. Christians have always believed that marriage is a uniting of our lives with one and only one person. It's a monogamous commitment between only two people, not three, four, or more.

But we need to understand that this requirement of exclusivity isn't tacked on to marriage as an afterthought. No, it's rooted in and flows from the one-flesh union. Because marriage is a comprehensive uniting of lives, it not only extends through time but must be total and complete at any given moment in time—that is, exclusive. And because it's a one-flesh union, this uniting of bodies sexually can only happen with two people, not three, four, or more.

Friendship is, naturally, a different kind of relationship. Friends share their lives with one another, and a close friendship can be quite intimate. But even close friends don't share their bodies with one another, at least not in a sexual way. You may help a friend move a piece of furniture or braid a friend's hair, but you shouldn't have intercourse with that person. Ironically, this "restriction" on friendship is what makes friendship special and beautiful. It's not a negative thing, because it means we don't have to limit our friendships to only one person, as we do in the case of a spouse. We can share our heart and mind with many people, and we can enjoy friendship with many people. This sharing of ourselves is what friendship is and one of the reasons it is wonderful to have friends. But because marriage involves sharing our body, as well as our heart and mind, it can only be done with one other person.

This is one reason that adultery is so devastating to marriage. You can share a meal or a car ride or a phone call with another person. But if you share your body, you will destroy your marriage. What we do with our bodies sexually matters.

This is also why polygamy is out of step with the biblical ideal of marriage as a one-flesh union. Sure, it happened in biblical times, but nowhere does it receive God's blessing or approval. And, yes, it happens today, but if you look closely, you find that the husband is not uniting himself completely to any one of his wives, precisely because he can't. Bodies can't be shared like that. Polygamy undermines the one-flesh union by robbing it of its mutuality. In fact, in most cultures that practice polygamy, men occupy the superior position in the relationship by giving only part of themselves, not their whole self, to any one of their wives. This is why polygamy is ultimately demeaning and degrading to women. The wives give themselves wholly to the husband, but the husband gives himself only partially to each of his wives.

When we move away from seeing marriage as a one-flesh union, we have no good reason to insist that marriage should be an exclusive union. Forsaking all others may suit your interests or be your personal preference, but without marriage as a one-flesh union, you will be hard-pressed to give a compelling reason why marriage should be exclusive. The exclusivity of marriage depends on the logic of a one-flesh union.

This is why most same-sex marriages tend not to be exclusive.[7] The most common, statistically speaking, are "open relationships" in which the partners agree to the terms of not being sexually exclusive. Gay activist Dan Savage recently referred to this as being "monogamish." Hanna Rosin, author of *The End of Men*, wrote a piece in *Slate* magazine titled "The Dirty Little Secret: Most Gay Couples Aren't Monogamous." She explains: "Gay couples are very different when it comes to sex, even if this is not the convenient moment to discuss that. And in legalizing gay marriage, we are accepting a form of sanctioned marriage that is not by habit monogamous and that is inventing all kinds of new models of how to accommodate lust and desire in long-term relationships."[8]

I share these quotes not to mock the idea of same-sex marriage, nor to suggest that same-sex monogamy is impossible. I am simply making the point that there is nothing inherent in a companionate view of marriage that requires monogamous exclusivity. If marriage is defined as a close emotional connection with another person where organic, bodily union (the kind that has the potential to produce offspring) doesn't matter, then there is no reason you can't share your body sexually with others, just like you might with a handshake or a hug.

## Permanence: Holding Fast to His Wife

When the idea of marriage as a comprehensive union goes away, so does the necessity of exclusivity. But that's not all we lose. A second characteristic that is threatened by the companionate view of marriage is *permanence*. We see this feature of marriage referenced in Genesis 2:24 as well: "That is why a man leaves his father and mother and is united to his wife." A man must hold fast to his wife. If exclusivity requires leaving—forsaking all others for an exclusive relationship with one person of the opposite sex—then permanence speaks to what is sometimes called cleaving, uniting "till death do us part." The Bible teaches, and Christians have always believed, that marriage should be marked by permanence—that you enter into a marital relationship not for a season but for life. As Jesus said, "Therefore what God has joined together, let no one separate" (Matthew 19:6).

Both exclusivity and permanence flow from the unique kind of relationship marriage is as a one-flesh union. Because marriage is a comprehensive uniting of lives, it demands that it be between only two persons (exclusive) and that this uniting be extended through time (permanent).[9]

Today, permanence is often seen as the most intimidating characteristic of marriage. That's why our culture is always finding ways to get around it. The most obvious product of these attempts has been "no-fault divorce," which has devastated a whole generation of men, women, and children.[10]

Yet, despite the tragic social consequences of widespread and easy divorce, some are proposing that we make things even easier and less complicated. One writer in the *Washington Post* recently advocated for marriages to work more like lease agreements, say, for a car. So, he says, we should move away from the notion of wedlock to the idea of "wedlease":

> Here's how a marital lease could work: Two people commit themselves to marriage for a period of years—one year, five years, 10 years, whatever term suits them. The marital lease could be renewed at the end of the term however many times a couple likes. It could end up lasting a lifetime if the relationship is good and worth continuing. But if the relationship is bad, the couple could go their separate ways at the end of the term. The messiness of divorce is avoided and the end can be as simple as vacating a rental unit.[11]

The rejection of permanence is also the reason we've seen a huge rise in the rate of cohabitation. Today 60 percent of first-time marriages begin with cohabitation, up from almost 0 percent fifty years ago. Many couples are afraid of getting "stuck" in a bad relationship or in the "wrong" relationship, so they try it out before committing. Sadly and ironically, this solution has the effect of further undermining their ability to enjoy a permanent, lasting marriage commitment. "Sexuality is a little like a post-it note," explains Sam Allberry. "And the more that union is forged and then broken, the more our capacity for deep and abiding unity is diminished."[12] So the proposed solution only makes the problem worse.[13] This is because cohabitating attempts a comprehensive union while removing an essential characteristic—permanence. This only serves to undermine the couple's ability to live together "till death do us part."

I fondly remember officiating the wedding of my cousin Anne to her fiancé Jason, and for me the most powerful moment in the service was the exchange of vows. What the bride and groom do in that moment forges the marriage covenant, as they give themselves to each other through publicly declared promises: "To have and to hold from this day forward, for better, for worse, for richer, for poorer, in sickness and health, to love and to cherish, until we are parted by death." They aren't promising to always feel a certain way, but to always remain faithful and to endure. Permanence is an essential feature of this one-flesh union. Without it, you don't have a biblical marriage.

## Biology, Not Bigotry

The Christian vision of marriage is a one-flesh union—a joining of two people, male and female, husband and wife, in a comprehensive union. Mere sexuality has defined marriage in this way—a way that is directly at odds with our culture today. Today, people think of marriage as an enduring commitment rooted in an emotional connection. A relationship that lasts . . . for a while . . . as long as I feel loving feelings toward you. Marriage isn't less than what we feel; it's just a lot more than that. It's a comprehensive union of heart, mind, soul, and body with one person for life—a one-flesh union in which the uniting of bodies matters, often issuing in the gift of children.

As we come more fully to appreciate the biblical rationale for marriage as a one-flesh union, I believe it will help us see and appreciate the rational basis for the Christian view of marriage. In our culture, an increasing number of people struggle with this view of marriage. But we also see an increasing number of people within the church, even the evangelical church, who are questioning this view of marriage. We have what I referred to earlier in this book as assertive advocates who believe that the historic and traditional view of marriage is wrong, and they would like to see the church change.

To the assertive advocates reading this, one of my hopes is that this short chapter will help you realize that the historic Christian view of marriage is rooted in biology, not bigotry. Those of us who maintain the historic Christian view of marriage—what I'm calling "mere sexuality"—do so not because we have any personal animus or hostility toward same-sex people, but because we believe bodies matter. And they matter immensely for marriage.

Let me also take a moment to speak to those who oppose same-sex marriage. What I would like to say to you is simple: Make sure you have a biblical and Christian view of marriage as a comprehensive one-flesh union. If you don't and if you embrace the way our culture defines marriage (as many

Christians do), then you have no good reason to oppose same-sex marriage, except that God says it's wrong. Of course, whatever God says is compelling in itself. But my point is that you won't have much to say to those outside the church about why God thinks same-sex marriage is wrong. At least, you won't have any publicly accessible reasons, the kind you could share with a non-Christian neighbor who is aghast that you don't embrace same-sex marriage and who doesn't accept the authority of the Bible.

If bodily union isn't an essential part of your definition of marriage, then you won't have a basis—again, apart from citing Scripture—for opposing same-sex marriage. If marriage is about finding your soul mate or sharing life together with your best friend, there's no reason two people of the same sex can't do that and be married according to your definition. Apart from quoting the Bible, your only argument against this type of marriage is, well, personal preference. My challenge to you is to come to terms with the moral logic undergirding the Christian vision of marriage. It's a view the church has advocated and embodied (albeit imperfectly) for centuries, and it is the only rationally consistent and publicly accessible way to defend marriage against attempts to change or redefine it.

## Christ's Permanent, Exclusive Commitment to His Bride

As important as it is to see both the biblical basis and the rational basis for the Christian view of marriage, it is even more important to understand the theological and Christological basis for marriage. What do I mean? We need to see that the one-flesh union between a man and a woman is rooted not just in biology but in God's redemptive plan for all of human history.

This is what we read in the book of Ephesians, as Paul describes the beauty of the one-flesh union of a man and a woman in marriage. Husbands ought to love and cherish their wives as much as they do their own bodies. So, too, wives ought to love and cherish their husbands. Paul then quotes a theme verse for this present chapter: "For this reason a man will leave his father and mother and be united to his wife, and the two will become one flesh" (5:31). But then Paul adds this—a surprising turn in the passage: "This is a profound mystery—but I am talking about Christ and the church." You see, marriage is hugely important, not only because of what it is, but also because of what it reflects. The one-flesh union of man and woman points to the union of Jesus Christ with his blood-bought bride, the church.

And just as permanence and exclusivity ought to mark our one-flesh union, so these same characteristics mark our Savior's commitment to us—his bride, the church. Permanence and exclusivity define our relationship with Christ. Having given his life for us on the cross, for our sins and for our salvation, our risen Savior now says to us, his bride, "Surely I am with you always, to the very end of the age" (Matthew 28:20), and "Never will I leave you; never will

I forsake you" (Hebrews 13:5). Jesus Christ, our Bridegroom, is the same yesterday, today, and forever! He is committed to us and loves us as his body in a relationship that is exclusive and will last forever.

# CHAPTER 5

# WHAT IS SEX FOR?

In this chapter, we will pivot to the topic of sex. The goal here is to think about the *purpose* of sex. Why do we have sex? Why does it exist? What I want you to understand from the start is that the companionate view of marriage, which we discussed in the last chapter, brings with it some ready-made answers to this question. But in the end, it doesn't give satisfying answers.

In the companionate view, sex is primarily for pleasure. Sounds good, right? The pleasure of sex serves to intensify the feeling of emotional connection you have with another person, so we might say that sex can help you feel more in love. According to our culture, this is the purpose of sex—*pleasure*.

You'll notice, however, that this purpose is very oriented to the individual. It focuses on what sex does for us—what we get out of it—and has little to do with the joining of two lives in a one-flesh union. It also doesn't have anything to do with creating life, that is, with making babies. In fact, any talk of procreation or making babies is explicitly excluded from our culture's understanding of sex. If you want evidence for this, take a close look at the Supreme Court's 2015 decision to legalize same-sex marriage in all fifty states.[1] Embedded in this ruling is the claim that marriage has no intrinsic connection to procreation and thus to children. On this view, marriage begins and ends with the interests of the partners, irrespective of any children who may come from that partnership. If you still doubt this, listen to one same-sex activist who anticipated the Court's decision with enthusiasm for precisely this reason. This legal ruling would, she says, shift the "institution's message" so that marriage ever after "will stand for sexual choice, for cutting the link between sex and diapers."[2]

Here is an example of where this trend is leading us. My wife recently received an email from a close friend with the following subject line: "You've got to read this!" Attached to the email was an article from a recent issue of *Vanity Fair*. It was titled "Tinder and the Dawn of the 'Dating Apocalypse.'" Perhaps you've never heard of Tinder. I hadn't. It's a dating app, like eHarmony, only it's less a dating app and more a hookup app. It's not about relationships; it's about sex. Which is why this writer sees Tinder and other hookup apps as the beginning of the end of dating as we know it. The article begins:

> It's a balmy night in Manhattan's financial district, and at a sports bar called Stout, everyone is Tindering. The tables are filled with young women and men

who've been chasing money and deals on Wall Street all day, and now they're out looking for hookups. Everyone is drinking, peering into their screens and swiping on the faces of strangers they may have sex with later that evening . . .

At a booth in the back, three handsome twenty-something guys in button-downs are having beers. They are Dan, Alex, and Marty, budding investment bankers at the same financial firm . . . When asked if they've been arranging dates on the apps they've been swiping at, all say not one date, but two or three: "You can't be stuck in one lane . . . There's always something better." . . .

[Alex, in fact] says that he himself has slept with five different women he met on Tinder—"Tinderellas," the guys call them—in the last eight days. Dan and Marty, also Alex's roommates in a shiny high-rise apartment building near Wall Street, can vouch for that. In fact, they can remember whom Alex has slept with in the past week more readily than he can.[3]

The article goes on like this for pages, unfolded with section headings that tell the story: "Sex Has Become So Easy," "Hit It and Quit It," "Boom-Boom-Boom Swipe," "The Morning After," and "People Are Gorging." It's all rather sobering stuff, a neo-pagan rather than deeply Christian approach to human sexuality.[4]

Sadly, though, the approach to sex described in this article isn't unique to users of Tinder or to millennials living in Manhattan. It's fairly routine practice on college campuses across the country, where hooking up has become a pastime.[5] But it's also common practice at younger ages. Did you know that, statistically speaking, half of all high school students will have sex before they graduate?

Sex has become so casual, so commercialized, so cheap, that it forces us to ask the most basic question: What is sex for? Does sex have any purpose beyond instant gratification? Does it have any higher meaning than, as advertisers would have it, to entice you to buy a new Cadillac or download the latest version of *Game of War* or pick up a case of Miller Lite on your way home from work?

## The Blessing of Sex

In the opening chapter of the book of Genesis, we discover the architecture for human sexuality, and what we find is that God has given humanity an amazing gift. As we saw in previous chapters, God created us in his image, not as single, solitary individuals, but as a sexually differentiated pair: "Male and female he created them" (1:27). Two creatures who are alike in so many ways, yet different. Alike in value and dignity, yet not alike in their bodies. They are sexually differentiated.

Then we read that having created them sexually differentiated as male and female, "God blessed them" (1:28). We could call this the blessing of sex, because it refers not only to the blessing of sexual difference as male and female, but to the blessing of our sexual powers: God has given us the marvelous and mysterious ability to unite two lives in a one-flesh union—to create new life. That's power indeed.[6]

Of course, with every gift God gives comes a corresponding call to use that gift to glorify God and bless others. Which is why God moves immediately from blessing the first human pair to calling them to action—a particular kind of action: "And God said to them, 'Be fruitful and increase in number; fill the earth and subdue it'" (1:28). At the heart of a biblical vision of sex is the bold affirmation that sex is a blessing. In our culture, sex may be viewed as a blessing because it feels good. But in the biblical vision, sex is a blessing not because of the pleasure it brings but because of the purpose it serves: to unite lives and to create life.[7]

For the Christian, then, sex has a dual purpose: to unite and to procreate. It serves to unite two lives in a one-flesh union and to bring forth new life from this one-flesh union. According to the Bible, this is the purpose of sex. This is what sex is for.

## When Sex Is Severed from Its Uniting and Procreating Purpose

Our culture has separated the act of sex from the purpose of sex. We have severed the connection between sex and its power to unite lives and create life, so that now, virtually everywhere we look, sex is separated from its uniting and procreating purpose. To put it bluntly, sex has been severed from both the institution of marriage and the blessing of having children.

How did this happen? The reasons are complex, but technology is one of the culprits. In particular, reproductive technologies, especially birth control, gained widespread acceptance in the sexual revolution of the 1960s and assisted in severing the link between the act of sex and the purpose of sex. In fact, this was one of the primary goals of the sexual revolution. Though it was euphemistically called "free love," in reality it meant consequence-free sex, or sex apart from commitments and children.

So how well did "free love" work out? Well, it hasn't been free. Our culture has paid the price, or more precisely, our children have paid it. We've had to bear the cost of "free love" with broken marriages and children growing up without the blessing of having a father and mother in a family. Another result of severing sex from its dual purpose of uniting lives and creating life has been the trivializing of sex. By robbing sex of its power to unite two lives and make life, we've turned sex into something far less powerful and profound than what it really is. It has become another recreational activity—a hobby, a consumer good, a plaything. As a culture, we're quickly growing bored with sex, even as we're gorging ourselves on it. Something has gone ludicrously wrong.

Even as we trivialize sex, we idolize pleasure, and sexual

gratification becomes a god. What is the multibillion-dollar-a-year porn industry other than the idolization of pleasure? Let's make no mistake about it, sexual pleasure, of all pleasures, is a highly addictive kind of pleasure.[8] The god of sexual pleasure has become a slave master—a demanding and unforgiving one that controls and destroys lives and relationships.

When we disconnect the act of sex from the purpose of sex, we also end up marginalizing children. When sex is simply a means for our personal pleasure, we see children as a problem, an inconvenience. Children are a "mistake" as we pursue our own agenda of pleasing ourselves. This mind-set threatens the well-being of children, who continue to come into this world, regardless of our wishes or desires, as a result of the act of sex. We call these "unwanted pregnancies," which is a euphemistic way of saying we want the pleasure of sex without the responsibility of creating new life. These are unwanted children, and the most blatant response to these so-called unwanted pregnancies is the blight on our national conscience known as abortion.

But that's not all. When we divorce sex from its purpose, we treat our body, or someone else's body, as though it were just a tool, something to be used by us or for us. This instrumentalizes the body in a way that distances us from our body and dis-integrates our sense of self. We inflict damage on ourselves without knowing it, using our bodies as instruments for pleasure rather than reverencing them as part and parcel of who we are.

In ancient Greece, the philosopher Aristotle described a slave as a "living tool."[9] This understanding of a person was roundly rejected by Christianity. How demeaning for a person created in the image of God to be seen as little more than an instrument for sexual pleasure! By divorcing sex from its God-given purpose, we harm ourselves and make it even harder to enjoy sex as a healthy experience of uniting lives for the sake of creating life.

## "'Course Sex Isn't Safe But It's Good"

This is why the Bible—and the Christian faith—insists that sexual activity should take place only within the context of marriage. Many people today, including those in the church, see the restriction of sexual activity to marriage as outdated—a puritanical limitation on our freedom. But the Bible teaches this, not to limit our joy of sex, but to increase it. We believe that sex is only for marriage, not because Christians are killjoys, but because we have a realistic and exalted view of the power of sex. Sex isn't a toy or plaything; it's a sacred and sovereign power—strong enough, in fact, to bring new life into being. When something is powerful—think of a downed power line or a loaded gun—you aren't careless when you handle it. You understand that it can kill or harm you if you aren't careful. Sex is a powerful creative gift, something God gives us for good purposes. But if we misuse it and are careless, it can profoundly harm us.

I remember standing at a crosswalk on Lake Street in

Oak Park, Illinois, a few hundred yards from the church I pastor. I was going out to grab a sandwich when I saw a woman, about my own age, staring at me. The look on her face was as if she'd been injured. She stopped me and asked if I was the pastor of the church. She mentioned that she'd visited several times. She then told me she'd just found out she was pregnant as the result of a one-night stand. I stood there, heartbroken with and for her, as she told me her story. It was sobering to think about the little immortal person, the new life, who had just been summoned into existence through her one-night stand.

Our sexual capacities are powerful, far too powerful to be used anywhere outside marriage. They need the safe and stable environment that comes with a "till death do us part" commitment. We need the uniting purpose of sex to safeguard us against the awesome procreative power of sex.

Unfortunately, we live in a world that has bought into the myth of "safe sex." But here's a news flash: there is no such thing as safe sex. Sex is too powerful ever to be safe. In the words of essayist Wendell Berry, "Sex was never safe, and it is less safe now than it has ever been."[10]

There is a famous scene in C. S. Lewis's *The Lion, the Witch and the Wardrobe* when Susan first hears about Aslan the lion, the Jesus figure in the story. Mr. Beaver needs to disabuse her of any misunderstanding about what this lion is like. "Aslan is a lion," explains Mr. Beaver, "*the* Lion, the great Lion." "Ooh!" says Susan. "I'd thought he was a man.

Is he—quite safe? I shall feel rather nervous about meeting a lion." "Safe?" says Mr. Beaver. "Who said anything about safe? 'Course he isn't safe. But he's good. He's the King, I tell you."[11]

Our culture often makes the same mistake as Susan. It confuses good and safe, assuming that because something is good, it must be safe. And so it asks, "Sex, is it—quite safe?" The hope is that sex will be simple and uncomplicated, free from consequences. "Yes, hook up with whomever you like, and don't worry!" But mere sexuality takes sex seriously and offers a realistic answer—graciously, yet honestly. "Safe? Who said anything about safe? 'Course sex isn't safe. But it's good. It's God's blessing to us, I tell you."

## Sex Has Public Consequences

When we acknowledge the procreative power of sex, we realize that sex cannot be simply reduced to a private act between consenting adults. Sex is an intrinsically public act. Why? Because it has massive public consequences. What are those consequences? One word: *children*.[12]

Many teenage couples have learned this the hard way. What begins as a fun high school romance turns into something more serious when a girl realizes she is pregnant. What they thought was something special and intimate, to be shared just between the two of them, has become something profoundly public and visible—not just to their parents or their families and friends or their classmates and teachers, but also to the son or daughter whose precious life they have inadvertently summoned into existence with their sexual powers—a child who no doubt will want to know one day when and where he or she came from. That's a public impact.

Sex isn't like other private acts. It's not the same as trimming your toenails, taking a shower, or flossing your teeth—all of which, I think you'll agree, are best done in private. Sex is like these other acts because it is done in private, yet it is profoundly different from these acts because it has a power that these other acts do not. You can never entirely sever sex from its public impact or significance. God has given us sexual powers to procreate, to bring another human being into existence, and this means that sex will always have a very public component to it.

Incidentally, this is the primary reason the state (our governing authorities) has any interest in marriage. It's worth asking: Why should the state have an interest in our sex lives? Again, if sex were like trimming your toenails, it would be ridiculous for the state to legislate on this activity. But again, we need to recognize that sex is different from other private acts. Sex has the power to bring forth other human beings—other members of the state who are granted certain rights as such. The state doesn't attempt to regulate our friendships; you don't need to go to the courthouse to sign a friendship certificate. But you do need state recognition when you get married. Why? Why should the state care about this at all? For the simple reason that marriages make babies, and this is of great interest to the state; indeed, therein lies the future of the state.

I hope you can see now why the state should have no interest in the sexual lives of same-sex couples. It's precisely because their sexual lives are, as a biological fact, sterile and nonprocreative. To put it bluntly, what two people of the same sex choose to do in their bedroom can have no lasting public significance because it cannot bring forth children. Of course, if that were the only concern we faced on this issue, it would be far easier to agree. The push we see today is not for allowance of private acts but for public recognition that seeks to redefine marriage in a way that discounts the procreative power it has to produce children.

Let me also say that this is why we want to promote, wherever and however we can, a strong marriage culture, both within the church and in our society. Marriage is the one institution that weds together the procreative and uniting purposes of sex in a powerful union. And when that happens, husbands win, wives win, and, most of all, children win.[13]

## Getting Personal

I recognize that for some, sex is a difficult topic to read about or discuss, for various reasons. Sex can be a great good when enjoyed as God intended, but it can also lead to pain. Sex has scarred quite badly some of you who are reading this. To even bring up the topic of sex is to tap into a host of painful experiences for you. I want to say to you that Jesus knows this about your experience, and he shares in the grief of it with you. He offers to heal you. He doesn't look on you with shame, and he won't turn you away in your guilt. He stands ready to forgive and receive you, whatever your past.

For others, the topic of sex evokes not pain, but longing. You would love to be married and to enjoy the benefits of sex and the joy of children, but you aren't currently married. You're single, and that's something you find disappointing, even frustrating. May I encourage you to continue to fight the fight of faith and trust God for his calling on your life, whether to marriage or to singleness. "'For I know the plans I have for you,' declares the LORD, 'plans to prosper you and not to harm you, plans to give you hope and a future'" (Jeremiah 29:11).

There are still others who are married and don't have kids—not by choice, but as a result of God's mysterious providence in their lives. Perhaps you're having trouble conceiving, and it has become a heavy burden for you. May I encourage you with the thought that the marital union you enjoy with your spouse is in itself intrinsically fruitful, even if the fruitfulness has not resulted in children. (Of course, adoption is also an option to prayerfully consider.)

Others reading this are married and may or may not have kids, but you're not sure you're up to doing the whole "kid thing." You look around at our culture, or you take stock of the pressures and demands of your own life or the challenges and practical burden of raising children, and you're not sure it's for you. I understand how you feel. I am reminded of the title of a *Time* magazine article—"The Economic Reason for Having Just One Child." The author points out that in 2011, the cost of raising a child to the age of eighteen was between $234,900 and $390,000.[14] And that amount didn't include college. I quickly did the math for my family of seven children, and it came out to several million dollars!

Wherever you are today, consider carefully that there are valid biblical reasons some may choose not to unleash their procreative sexual powers. But we always need to be open, at least in principle, to the procreative purpose of our one-flesh union. We should be careful not to use birth control to control God in a way that misses out on God's greater blessing for our lives in the form of children.[15] And let us not forget what Scripture clearly says about children—something profoundly and wonderfully countercultural: "Children are a heritage from the LORD, offspring a reward from him" (Psalm 127:3).

Finally, let us not lose sight of our Savior's own attitude toward children: "Let the little children come to me, and do not hinder them, for the kingdom of God belongs to such as these" (Mark 10:14). Every husband and wife should adopt a similar openness toward children, especially those who would be the fruit of their one-flesh sexual union.

## Marriage and Mission

In our hypersexualized culture, Christians should be at the forefront in championing a radically different vision of sex. We should insist that sex has a higher, nobler purpose than simply our pleasure. Of course we agree that sex is pleasurable—and Christians should be the first to say so! Remember, God is the author of every creaturely pleasure. But Christians should also insist, thoughtfully and respectfully, that pleasure isn't the sole or even primary purpose of sex. God has made us male and female, in our sexual difference and with our unique sexual powers, so that we might unite our lives and create new life. Sex has a splendid purpose.

Yet as important as the procreative and uniting purposes of sex are, these aren't the ultimate end for which God has given us either sex or marriage. Both sex and marriage have a greater missional purpose: the advance of the kingdom of God. Or as Christopher Ash has put it in his excellent book on this theme, sex is to be "in the service of God."[16] As we read in the opening chapter of Genesis, "God blessed them and said to them, 'Be fruitful and increase in number; fill the earth and subdue it. Rule over the fish in the sea and the birds in the sky and over every living creature that moves on the ground" (1:28).

I appreciate what famed professor of preaching William H. Willimon says about "the blessed burden" of bearing children in today's topsy-turvy world: "In a world plagued by self-doubt and uncertainty coupled with selfishness and irresponsibility which may arise from doubts and uncertainties, the bearing of children as a bold, conscious faithful response to God's offer of new life may become an evangelistic, even missional activity, a bold vulnerability which springs from faith."[17]

He goes on to press a question we're all tempted to ask: "The question is recurrently being phrased, 'Can I, with the world in the shape it is in, responsibly bring children into this kind of world?'" But as he says, "The question ought to be (for those who see children as a gift and the world as their responsibility), 'Can I, with the world in the shape it is in, responsibly refuse to bring children into this kind of world?'"[18]

How will you answer that question?

# CHAPTER 6

# FRIENDSHIP, CELIBACY, AND SAME-SEX RELATIONSHIPS

We've looked at the why of sex and how sex relates to marriage, but now we need to address the most difficult, sensitive, and controversial implication of the vision of human sexuality outlined in this book. I should also add, though, that it is perhaps the strongest argument in support of same-sex relationships.

As we've seen, the Bible affirms that human beings are sexually differentiated, male and female, and this defines what marriage is and what sex is for. Marriage is a one-flesh union built on the sexual complementarity of male and female—a uniting of heart, mind, and body. And within this view of marriage, sex is intended to unite two lives and create new life. Sex has both a unitive and a procreative purpose.

So far, so good. But controversial implications follow

from this. Put positively, all sexual activity ought to express and embody the one-flesh union we call marriage, for this is the God-given purpose of sex. Put negatively, any form of sexual activity that fails to express or embody a one-flesh union is out of step with the teaching of Scripture and outside the will of God.

Let me put it this way. According to the Bible and the nearly unanimous consensus of the church—what we're calling "mere sexuality"—God says Yes! to the sexual difference of male and female, Yes! to the joining of lives to form a one-flesh union called marriage, and Yes! to enjoying the unitive and procreative powers of sex—a divine hearty Yes! to it all. There's nothing wrong or sinful or disordered about any of this, and there's everything right and good and glorious about all of it.

But with this Yes! comes an equally resolute No! Because, according to the Bible and the nearly unanimous consensus of the Christian church, God says No! to any and every form of sexual activity outside of this one-flesh union called marriage. And let me hasten to add that God says No! irrespective of the sex of the people involved, whether same sex or opposite sex.

Let me stop to emphasize this point. The Bible is clear, as has been the centuries-old teaching of the Christian church, that same-sex sexual activity is out of step with God's will for human beings. But the church has held this position, not because it hates same-sex sexual activity, but because this is sexual activity outside of the one-flesh union of marriage. Biblically speaking, the sex of the two people engaging in the sexual act isn't the main issue. The main problem with same-sex activity is that it happens outside of the legitimate one-flesh union designed exclusively for the covenant of marriage. Simply put, sexual activity is inappropriate for anyone—male or female, same-sex- or opposite-sex-attracted—outside of the context of the one-flesh union we call marriage.

## Celibacy and the Prospect of Lifelong Loneliness

This position of "no sexual activity outside of a one-flesh union in marriage" is a difficult position for any of us to embrace. But it is especially difficult for persons who experience consistent same-sex attraction. It would seem to leave same-sex-attracted individuals with no legitimate, biblically sanctioned means of expressing their sexual desires—a daunting thought indeed.

However, I would suggest that it is this seemingly unnecessary or even unjust burden imposed on same-sex people that provides perhaps the strongest argument against mere sexuality. How so? For a simple reason: God's No! to sexual intimacy apart from marriage means, at least for consistently same-sex-attracted Christians, the high likelihood of lifelong celibacy and with that the prospect of lifelong loneliness.

Consider that for a moment. Let the full weight of what this implies sink in. In chapter 2, I shared the story of Justin

Lee, a same-sex-attracted Christian who has come to the conclusion that sexual intimacy among same-sex-attracted people can in certain circumstances be blessed by God. Much of the persuasive power of his story works at the gut level; that is to say, in reading his story, it is easy to conclude that denying Justin the right to enjoy the same privileges of intimacy and marriage others enjoy seems like cruel and unusual punishment, even a kind of torture.

So we need to take that concern seriously. But let's take a look at another story as well. I've already shared about my friend Wesley Hill, who likewise is consistently same-sex-attracted, but who comes to a very different conclusion from Justin on same-sex sexual activity. Wesley affirms mere sexuality and the church's historic teaching on this. Like Justin, Wesley doesn't sugarcoat what this means for him personally. In fact, he's very honest about his fear of trying to live a celibate life as a same-sex-attracted Christian. Listen to this candid confession: "What I feared most, though, about my decision to remain celibate was that I had thereby doomed myself to lifelong loneliness."[1]

If you are married, especially if you've been married for a while, you may have a hard time empathizing with Wesley's fear. In fact, if you're honest, you might think to yourself, *I'd like to enjoy the single life for a few weeks!* You might appreciate the peace and quiet, the ability to come and go as you please. But take a moment to listen to Wesley Hill unpack the bleak reality of lifelong loneliness.

When I was still in high school, despite being gay, I often daydreamed about what it would be like to be married, to have a house and children, to have a home of the sort I had growing up, to know that I belonged somewhere. Now, in light of where I felt my Christian faith was taking me, I stopped dreaming about those things. In their place, I began to have a recurrent picture of myself around age sixty, coming home to an empty apartment, having lived all of my adulthood as a single man. I started to think about the particulars of that scenario: not knowing each year where I'd be for Christmas, waking up each morning to a quiet bedroom and having no one across the table from me as I ate my cereal before heading to work, coming home at the end of the day and reading a book with no one to talk to about the parts of it that stood out to me. I began to resonate with what Lauren Winner has called "the loneliness of the everyday": "the loneliness of no one knowing if your plane lands on time, of no one to call if you lock yourself out of your house or your alternator dies—I find that loneliness worse [than the loneliness that comes as a result of a breakup or a divorce]."[2]

## Restoring Friendship to Its Rightful Place

What I appreciate about Wesley's and Justin's stories is that they're both brutally honest. Reading their stories ought to be challenging for all of us who enjoy the blessing of marriage, or even the prospect of marriage. So what do we say to someone like Wesley who because of biblical conviction is committed to lifelong celibacy? Does the church have anything to say other than, "Sorry, that's just the price of being consistently same-sex-attracted"? What can we do to address this very real dilemma for him and thousands of others like him?

There are many answers to that question, but at least one thing the church can and should do is to work to restore friendship to its rightful place in our lives and in our relationships in the church. As Christians and as a faith community, we can prioritize those deep, intimate, affectionate, nonsexual relationships we call friendships. We can work to strengthen the friendship culture of the church so that the church becomes a relationally thick and rewarding place— not just for married folks, but for singles, even celibates, like my friend Wesley Hill.

In short, we can recover the Bible's vision for spiritual friendship—a vision of human connection in which soul is knit to soul, united together in Christ-honoring love for one another. We need to read, study, and talk about the robust view of the Bible regarding same-sex relationships. The Bible doesn't call these relationships marriages, and they don't involve sexual activity. It calls them friendships: deep, intimate, nonsexual relationships.[3]

Consider the friendship of David and Jonathan. While not the only example of friendship in the Bible, their relationship is surely one of the most famous. We won't take time here to trace the story line, but a good look at the language of these verses should make the point clear:

> After David had finished talking with Saul, Jonathan became one in spirit with David, and he loved him as himself. From that day Saul kept David with him and did not let him return home to his family. And Jonathan made a covenant with David because he loved him as himself. Jonathan took off the robe he was wearing and gave it to David, along with his tunic, and even his sword, his bow and his belt.
>
> 1 SAMUEL 18:1–4

Notice the brief but powerful description of friendship in these verses. We see genuine intimacy, commitment, affection, sacrifice, even the exchange of vows. This is not unlike a marriage in terms of the strength of the bond.

But the most moving testimony to their friendship is seen when David offers his eulogy at Jonathan's death.

> "How the mighty have fallen in battle!
>    Jonathan lies slain on your heights.
> I grieve for you, Jonathan my brother;
>    you were very dear to me.
> Your love for me was wonderful,
>    more wonderful than that of women."
>
> 2 SAMUEL 1:25–26

The Bible envisions an intimacy and affection, indeed a

love, with as much or more potency than the romantic bond between husband and wife. Not because it's erotic, as some progressive Bible scholars have tried to suggest, but because it involves a genuine union of heart and mind, a knitting of soul to soul. It requires mutual commitment and sacrificial service for each other's good. This is a powerful covenantal bond, and it is something we need to recover in the church today—a robust understanding of same-sex friendship.

## A Weak Friendship Culture Makes Celibacy Much Harder

David and Jonathan enjoyed a profoundly intimate and enduring friendship. Jesus and the beloved disciple John also enjoyed such a friendship. And it's what Jesus envisions for all of his followers—a community of friendship, in fact. He said, "I no longer call you servants . . . Instead, I have called you friends" (John 15:15).

Just imagine for a moment if this kind of friendship was common in the church rather than rare. What would it do to elevate all of our relationships, and especially to lift the spirits of the single and celibate among us?

The reality, however, is that deep friendships, like the one between Jonathan and David, are hard to find. I'm not talking about having a few buddies you exchange emails or texts with, or colleagues you connect with on LinkedIn or Facebook. I'm talking about deep, intimate, affectionate, lasting, nonsexual relationships that people living in other centuries recognized as friendships.

American culture has lost this. The church, too, suffers from a weak friendship culture. So it is with the church as well. Friendship has been eclipsed by our obsession with sex and sexual activity. There are multiple reasons for this trend, no doubt, but I'll point to two key factors. On the one hand, we as a culture have elevated the romantic relationship as the most fulfilling relationship possible—the supreme relationship that trumps all others. Friendship tends to pale in comparison—unless, that is, you have a friendship "with benefits." But then it's no longer a friendship; it has turned into something else.

On the other hand, we're convinced as a culture that marriage is an all-sufficient relationship, one that can and will meet all our relational needs. Consider this fascinating statistic. Did you know that most people stop forming deep friendships after the age of twenty-eight? And do you know what else tends to happen, on average, around the age of twenty-eight? People get married. Just a coincidence? I don't think so.

In the companionate view of marriage, your spouse is your best friend. This means your spouse does double duty in your life. He or she is both your spouse and your best friend. And this expectation places a great burden on marriage and leaves little room for other friendships that might "compete" with your relationship with your spouse.

What is the net result of our weak friendship culture, especially for same-sex-attracted Christians? It leaves them with little real opportunity to enjoy healthy, meaningful connection with others in the church. Or to put it differently, it leaves same-sex-attracted and celibate Christians in a relational no-man's-land of isolation and loneliness, with very few, if any, others with whom they can forge meaningful, enduring relationships.

## Singles Aren't Single in the Body of Christ

But this weak friendship culture isn't just an issue for consistently same-sex-attracted celibate Christians. It's a challenge for anyone who is single. And it means that if Christians are going to make headway on this issue with gay celibate Christians, we have to reimagine what it means to be single. This starts with the realization that singles aren't single in the body of Christ. Those who are not married should remain chaste sexually, and some may be called to a life of celibacy. But in a very real sense, single Christians are never single. They are united to Christ, and because of this union they are united, inextricably, to every other person in the body of Christ.

Singleness isn't a particularly biblical idea. In fact, the language of being single assumes that marriage is the preferred norm, which it isn't. It also adopts an unhealthy idea from American individualism by suggesting that we are, at the core of our identity, autonomous selves, while the Bible suggests otherwise. Insofar as the church is unwelcoming to singles, whether same-sex-attracted or not, or, worse yet, shallow and superficial in its relationships with singles, this is what will likely happen: single people will look elsewhere for community. And if they are same-sex-attracted, that "elsewhere" may be the welcoming embrace of the gay subculture.

The church is supposed to be a community of friends—of spiritual friendship. We hope for thousands of David and Jonathan–like relationships, not simply a weekly meeting place for autonomous individualists who happen to show up at the same time. God's purpose is for the church is to be a community where water is thicker than blood.[4] That is, where the waters of baptism reflect our union in Christ as brothers and sisters, as a single family, bound together with spiritual ties that transcend and outlast any familial, blood connections.

Jesus was clear on this point. When his mother and brothers decided to do a first-century-style family intervention on him, worried that he had gone a bit over the top in his ministry output, they tracked him down at a crowded house where he was teaching. They called for him to come outside to his family. In response, as he looked out over the crowd, Jesus said something that doesn't exactly square with our Christian culture of focusing on the family: "'Who are my mother and my brothers?' he asked. Then he looked at those seated in a circle around him and said, 'Here are my mother and my brothers! Whoever does God's will is my brother and sister and mother'" (Mark 3:33–35). Jesus taught that the ties that bind us together are thicker than blood. They are sealed in the waters of baptism when we confess Christ as Lord and pledge to do God's will.

And yet in the Christian community, where water is thicker than blood, it is still true—in a different sense—that blood is thickest of all. Not the blood that binds us biologically, but the blood that binds us eternally. I'm talking about the blood of Christ—the blood shed for you and me for the remission of our sins. It is the blood that flows from the wounds by which we are healed, the blood "that speaks a better word than the blood of Abel" (Hebrews 12:24), the blood that poured forth from Jesus' hands and his side as he cried in seeming abandonment, "My God, my God, why have you forsaken me?" (Mark 15:34).

This blood, the blood of the Lamb, is thickest of all. Which means that all of us who have washed ourselves in the blood of the Lamb now enjoy union with our Savior and communion with one another, a profound spiritual connection that goes deeper than any other.

## A Place for Love

I want to share a final reflection about my friend Wesley Hill, a same-sex-attracted Christian who believes he is called to sexual chastity and celibacy. Wesley had to confront his fear of lifelong loneliness, but over time, the issue changed for him, prompting him to ask a different question: Is there a place for my love—to love and to be loved as a same-sex-attracted Christian?

He writes about this shift movingly in his book *Spiritual Friendship*: "My primary question, over time, became a question about love. Where was I to find love? Where was I to *give* love? If Scripture and the Christian tradition were right that I shouldn't try to find a husband, surely the apparent corollary couldn't also be right—that I was therefore cut off from any deep, meaningful form of intimacy and communion. Could it?"[5]

Perhaps you are a same-sex-attracted Christian, and you've asked yourself that question many times. Or maybe this is the first time you've thought about it, and it speaks to a hidden longing in your soul. Perhaps you are not same-sex-attracted, but you're single, and you can relate to the longing to find a place for your love—to love and to be loved, even without a spouse.

After sitting with this question for some time, Wesley gestures in the direction where he hopes to find an answer:

There *is*, in fact, a place for love, and it's called friendship.

As someone trying to reconcile his Christian faith with his homosexuality, I have become increasingly drawn to that notion: that there exists, for someone like me, a location for my love. That, by rediscovering ancient, and not-so-ancient, forms and exemplars of friendship, I might be able to rewrite the lonely future

I feared would be my lot as a celibate gay Christian.
That I too am called to nurture, deepen, and sanctify
my love."[6]

Could the church, as Wesley hopes, rediscover this lost
expression of love? Could it become the kind of community
that is a place for same-sex love and friendship? Isn't that a
marvelous, countercultural vision?

Elsewhere Wesley writes about his hope for this to be
true of the church:

I imagine a future in the church when the call
to chastity would no longer sound like a dreary sentence to lifelong loneliness for a gay Christian like me.
I imagine Christian communities in which friendships are celebrated and honored—where it's normal
for families to live near or with single people; where
it's expected that celibate gay people would form significant attachments to other single people, families,
and pastors; where it's standard practice for friends to
spend holidays together or share vacations; where it's
not out of the ordinary for friends to consider staying
put, resisting the allure of constant mobility, for the
sake of their friendships. I imagine a church where genuine love isn't located exclusively or even primarily in
marriage, but where marriage and friendship and other
bonds of affection are all seen as different forms of the
same love we all are called to pursue.[7]

He summarizes with these poignant words, a challenge for each of us, regardless of our marital status or sexual orientation: "Not everyone can be a parent or a spouse, but anyone and everyone can be a friend."[8] To which, I trust, we all will say, "Yes!" and "Amen!"

## CHAPTER 7

# HOMEWARD BOUND

Now that we've looked at the common and core beliefs of the Christian faith with regard to sexuality—this mere sexuality—I want to show how all of this connects to eternity and to ethics. In other words, I want to connect sexuality to hope and to holiness by showing that there is a way of life (ethics) that corresponds to our practice of mere sexuality and to the future that God has in store for us (eschatology). And this is captured in one simple but surprisingly elusive word: *patience*.

If we're not able to wait patiently, we won't be able to live within the teaching of mere sexuality. Almost every departure or deviation from mere sexuality is an expression of our impatience. We don't want to wait for what God has promised, or we refuse to live within the parameters God has designed.

But let's be honest for a moment. We all struggle with patience, don't we? We want what we want, and we want it now, thank you very much! We live in a culture of excess and instant gratification. Soon enough, flying drones will be delivering items to our doorstep an hour after we order them! In this culture, we have a hard time waiting for much of anything, not least the good things God gives to us in our sexuality.

This struggle is not limited to the secular culture; Christians also struggle with impatience. We're not immune to our instant-gratification culture, and we can be impatient with God's design for sexuality or with his provision for us sexually. Consider a few statistics that demonstrate this: According to a 2014 report by Christian Mingle and JDate, 61 percent of Christians say they would have sex before marriage; 56 percent say it's okay to move in with someone after dating between six months and two years.[1] These are telltale signs of our impatience. We don't like to wait.

I'm not sitting on a soapbox clucking my tongue at this reality. I get it! I remember battling with impatience as a college freshman. I desperately wanted to get married to my high school sweetheart. We had been dating for several years and knew we wanted to get married. And I was convinced now was the time. So I sat down with her father to float the idea by him and get his read. Katie's father wasn't nearly as convinced of the timing as I was! "Are you close to finishing college?" he asked. "No." "Have you ever earned a real paycheck?" "No." "Well, come see me in a few years." For the record, he wasn't quite that gruff. But he was clearly saying to me, "Todd, now is not the right time. Be patient."

## Waiting Patiently in Hope

Those weren't easy words for me to hear. They never are, because patience is painful—not least in our sexual lives. Being patient means we're going to have to bear up under some kind of burden or embrace something we'd rather not have to endure. In short, it's going to involve some measure of suffering.

That is why we need to sink our teeth into the glorious text of Romans 8. This passage gives us a worldview that makes sense of the suffering that patience brings and reminds us that our lives as human beings—and by implication as sexual beings—will involve suffering. Paul speaks of "our present sufferings" (8:18). Suffering is an inescapable feature of this fallen world. In our lives as human beings and as sexual beings, we will experience futility and frustration—various forms of unwanted and sometimes intense suffering. No one will have a problem-free existence. Don't be surprised, then, if you find you're having difficulty with your sexuality. That's normal—sadly normal.

But we also learn from this passage that it is okay to groan inwardly because of the pain we experience and the longing we feel. I love the realism of this passage: "We ourselves, who have the firstfruits of the Spirit, groan inwardly as we wait eagerly for our adoption to sonship" (Romans 8:23). Paul doesn't deny that we groan. We want relief from the struggle, and we want satisfaction for our desire. And waiting for either of these—relief from pain or satisfaction of desire—is hard. It makes us groan inwardly.

But this passage also holds out hope that the redemption of our bodies will mean the cessation of our suffering. We who have the firstfruits of the Spirit "groan inwardly," Paul says, "as we wait eagerly for our adoption to sonship, the redemption of our bodies" (8:23). If we've put our faith in Christ, we've been adopted into God's family. But the fullness of that adoption has not yet come—there is still more. And this "more" is the redemption of our bodies, which, when it happens at the resurrection, will remove all our scars, heal all our wounds, and mend all our brokenness.

In the end, we see that what awaits us in glory far surpasses anything we lack in this life. Paul writes, "I consider that our present sufferings are not worth comparing with the glory that will be revealed in us" (Romans 8:18). If you had a scale to weigh your sufferings against the glory to come, there would be no comparison. Absolutely none. And that's Paul's punch line: we wait patiently in hope for this glory.

## The Possibility of Healing, the Promise of Redemption

As Christians we struggle to be patient not only with God's designs for our sexuality, but also with God's provision for our sexual brokenness. We want what we want, and we want it now. We want the messy parts of our lives to be fixed, and fixed now. Instant healing, please, and no muddled process to get there, thank you very much!

Consider the story of my friend Joel, which you can learn more about in the second appendix. His story is one of brokenness and pain. It doesn't yet have an "I found Jesus and all is well" ending. He is still living with unresolved issues. We tend to prefer stories with happy endings: the person is miraculously freed from his or her burdens and—voilà—completely healed. We like these stories, and we call them "testimonies." But stories with large parts unresolved make us nervous. Why? Because we're impatient with the healing process.

In saying this, I don't want to pooh-pooh the possibility of healing in this life, nor do I deny the power of God's grace to change lives radically and even suddenly. God is in that sort of business, and when it happens, it is indeed glorious! Take the story of Melinda Selmys, author of a vulnerable yet theologically rich book about her journey with her own sexuality titled *Sexual Authenticity*. She describes herself as a lesbian, feminist, and atheist who miraculously found Christ. Now she's a homeschooling mother of four. Quite a transformation! She rightly says the change in her life is "more improbable than the Himalayas deciding, one summer morning, to get their trunks on and go for a swim."[2] We should praise God for such profound change!

But notice the way she describes her healing. What did she find that made the difference?

A young gay man once asked me how I had come to change from a homosexual into a heterosexual. I didn't know how to answer him, because the question seemed strange and remote. Heterosexuality had nothing to do with it. I went from being an atheist, struggling along in a godless and unforgiving world, desperately trying to cobble together meaning from the scraps of glory that my nihilistic worldview hadn't yet explained away, to being a Christian. I didn't find the secret path out of never-never land that leads to the straight world, or the fountain of heterosexuality; I found Christ.[3]

That's the key. We may not find all the healing we want in this life, but we can know Christ—and be known by him. And we can trust Christ with the process of healing and with our hope for the future—and present—redemption of our bodies. Christians ought always to hope in the God who heals. But they should do so soberly, as those who recognize that their path of discipleship may be tenderly appointed with a thorn in the flesh (2 Corinthians 12:7)—not as a punishment, but as a means of grace: "My grace is sufficient for you, for my power is made perfect in weakness" (12:9).

## Homeward Bound

Without a doubt, my favorite book series of all time is J. R. R. Tolkien's *The Lord of the Rings*. If you've seen the movies but never read the books, all I can say is that you've done yourself a disservice. The books are full of endearing characters and spellbinding adventure, and I love the elegantly described scenes with their marvelous dialogue. One such scene comes near the end of the final book, in one of the closing chapters titled "Homeward Bound." The One Ring has been destroyed, Sauron vanquished, and Aragorn enthroned, and now the hobbits are on their return journey to the Shire.

At last the hobbits had their faces turned towards home. They were eager now to see the Shire again; but at first they rode only slowly, for Frodo had been ill at ease. When they came to the Ford of Bruinen, he had halted, and seemed loth to ride into the stream; and they noted that for a while his eyes appeared not to see them or things about him. All that day he was silent. It was the sixth of October.

"Are you in pain, Frodo?" said Gandalf quietly as he rode by Frodo's side.

"Well, yes I am," said Frodo. "It's my shoulder. The wound aches, and the memory of darkness is heavy on me. It was a year ago today."

"Alas! There are some wounds that cannot be wholly cured," said Gandalf.

"I fear it may be so with mine," said Frodo. "There is no real going back. Though I may come to the Shire, it will not seem the same; for I shall not be the same. I am wounded with knife, sting, and tooth, and a long burden. Where shall I find rest?"

Gandalf did not answer.[4]

Indeed, Gandalf didn't need to answer. Because both he and Frodo knew where they were headed. They were homeward bound. They were headed, not just back to the Shire, the home of the hobbits, but to the Grey Havens, that place of perfect rest and peace where every wound finds healing, every pain finds comfort, and every longing finds satisfaction and joy.

## "Be Patient toward All That Is Unsolved in Your Heart"

Throughout this book, I've referred numerous times to my friend Wesley Hill and to his profound book so aptly titled *Washed and Waiting*. I can't commend it to you highly enough. Wesley says that as he was writing his book, which is a very intimate account of his personal struggles, he taped onto his desk a quote from the German poet Rainer Maria Rilke: "Be patient toward all that is unsolved in your heart."

That, in a single sentence, is the way of life that corresponds to mere sexuality: patience toward all that is unsolved in your heart. Patiently waiting for joy, as Paul puts it in Romans 8: "Who hopes for what they already have? But if we hope for what we do not yet have, we wait for it patiently" (verses 24–25).

Listen to Wesley explain the significance of this Rilke quote for his own story, and see if it doesn't speak to your story as well: "Having patience with your own weakness is, I think, something of what Paul was commending when he described the tension of living on this side of wholeness. When God acts climactically to reclaim the world and raise our dead bodies from the grave, there will be no more homosexuality. But until then, we hope for what we do not see."[5]

Indeed, on that day not only will there be no more homosexuality; there will be no more desires of any kind that are out of step with God's design for human beings. There will be no more longings of any kind that are not met fully in seeing the face of our Lord Jesus Christ. On that day, all will be well, all will be whole, all will be joy!

And so we wait for it patiently, in hope.

# CASTING VISION WITH JOY, TEARS, AND HOPE

I've written this book to help you rediscover "mere sexuality"—the biblical and historic Christian vision of human sexuality. But our task must go beyond recovering a lost vision. If we're going to reverse the downward slide of evangelical Christianity into a neo-pagan sexuality, then we need to cast vision for mere sexuality. We need to recover this vision for our own sake and then advocate for it for the sake of others—as an exercise in pastoral persuasion, speaking convincingly into our contemporary context.

Casting vision goes beyond the work of scholarship and touches on the need for winsome communication. We need more than sound exegesis and good theology; we need compelling Christian rhetoric and prose and poetry. Our challenge is not only to convince minds but also to capture imaginations. We want people to see the truth of God's design for human sexuality, but also its goodness and its beauty. Taking a cue from theologian and cultural critic Carl Trueman, we need to win the aesthetic, not just the argument. As he puts it, "Arguments can be true or false, good or bad. But today who cares? We live in an age where the primary moral binary is between the tasteful and distasteful. Control of aesthetics is where the real power to change people lies."[1]

How do we do that? Well, I don't presume to have all the answers or even a silver bullet. But if our vision casting for God's design for human sexuality is going to be effective, it must be done with joy, with tears, and with hope.

We cast vision with *joy*, as those who are ravished by the beauty of mere sexuality, not just convinced of the truth of it. The rising generation of evangelicals needs to encounter both the rational coherence of the Christian vision of sexuality and its moral and aesthetic beauty. Here we can take a cue from C. S. Lewis, who early on in his career realized that rational argument would take a person only so far. What was ultimately needed, he insisted, was a baptized imagination.[2] This is why Lewis not only wrote *The Abolition of Man* but followed it with his Space Trilogy series of novels, fleshing out some of the very same points. He later explained that "by casting all these things into an imaginary world, stripping them of their stained-glass and Sunday school associations, one could make them for the first time appear in their real potency."[3] That's a wonderful description of what is required for us to commend the beauty of mere sexuality: to make it appear for the first time in its real potency, whether in our preaching, our tweets, or our songs—or better yet, as an embodied reality in our own lives.

But our vision casting also needs to be done with *tears*, sharing with others in the heartbreaking complexity of these issues. There is a lovely gentleman in our congregation, a godly man in his early sixties, who wakes up most mornings wishing he were a woman. He has had these desires most of his life, starting when he was just five years old. I weep with him in his struggle.

Or consider the email I recently received from a young couple who had been thinking about moving to Chicago and attending our church. Their dreams and plans were interrupted with the birth of their first child, who was born with female genitals but an XY chromosome—a rare medical condition known as intersex. This precious young couple didn't even know what intersex was until they had a child born with the condition.

These are the stunningly complex and often heartbreaking situations of people in our world and in our churches. They're not "issues" to be solved, but people to be loved, even to the point of weeping with those who weep, shedding tears of grief and sadness with them. We will not communicate a faithful and compelling vision for mere sexuality if our posture is overly muscular and not sufficiently brokenhearted.

Finally, if our efforts are going to be effective, we need to cast this vision with *hope*, as those who believe in the future promise of the gospel—that while we experience a measure of healing in this life, complete transformation will occur in the life to come. This promise is grounded not in the righteousness of our sexual propriety, but in the death and resurrection of Jesus Christ—and it is true for even the chief of sinners.

Ultimately, each of us needs to know in the depth of our soul that "there is no one righteous, not even one . . . All have turned away, they have together become worthless; there is no one who does good, not even one" (Romans 3:10, 12); that "a person is not justified by works of the law," or by his heterosexuality, but only "through faith in Jesus Christ" (Galatians 2:16 ESV); that we all deal with sexual struggles of one kind or another; that we all need forgiveness and healing for our sexual sin; and that Jesus is more than willing to meet us there—in our brokenness, in our shame, in our sin.

"Here I am!" Jesus says. "I stand at the door and knock. If anyone hears my voice and opens the door, I will come in and eat with that person, and they with me" (Revelation 3:20). Most importantly, we need to know that as we open the door of our lives to Christ Jesus our Savior, he will indeed humbly enter in—bringing with him all of his grace and beauty and power—washing us, sanctifying us, and justifying us in his own glorious name!

# FOUR CORE SCRIPTURAL CONVICTIONS

My strong appeal in this book to the importance of the retrieval of Christian tradition should not be taken as an attempt to sidestep the foundational role of Scripture in driving mere sexuality. There are, of course, strong biblical convictions that undergird this vision. Lengthy biblical exposition is not the purpose of this book; others have done the job admirably. But here I would like to highlight just four scriptural convictions and root them in a single passage: 1 Corinthians 6:9–11. These convictions can be traced to many other texts, but this one is helpful because it's short and clear.

The first conviction is simple. *Sexuality matters, because what you do with your body sexually can determine your destiny eternally.* Certain sexual practices can shut you out of the kingdom of God. This is the startling truth Paul wanted the Corinthians to understand:

> Or do you not know that wrongdoers will not inherit the kingdom of God? Do not be deceived: Neither the sexually immoral nor idolaters nor adulterers nor men who have sex with men nor thieves nor the greedy nor drunkards nor slanderers nor swindlers will inherit the kingdom of God.
>
> 1 CORINTHIANS 6:9–10

For many people today, sex is seen as no big thing—a recreational activity that consenting adults choose to enjoy, something of little or no consequence or even significance, sort of like watching a movie together (or as some might say today, "Let's Netflix and chill"). The Bible sees sexuality differently. I like the way author Kevin DeYoung puts it: "It cannot be overstated how seriously the Bible treats the sin of sexual immorality."[1] Precisely. Scripture says sexual practice matters forever.

Following this is the second conviction. *There are two ways to express our sexuality as Christians: mere sexuality or sexual immorality.* There is the way God designed our sexuality to function, and then there is every other way that is disordered and deviates from God's good intentions. Paul flags several sinful practices that shut one out of the kingdom of God. Topping the list is a Greek word (*pornoi*) that serves as an umbrella term for lots of things and refers in this context to those who practice any kind of sexual immorality. Note that adultery and homosexual practice are but two expressions of this immorality; there are also others that fall outside mere sexuality and can exclude one from the kingdom. The point is that there are not just shades of gray but a stark moral clarity. For the Christian who wants to live faithfully in this world, there are only two options: sexual immorality or mere sexuality.

A third conviction brings some balance to these first two. *We need to remember that sexual sins aren't the only serious sins.* Sometimes Christians are criticized for seeming to be overly obsessed with sexual sin. Critics sometimes wonder if our concerns are just a bad hangover from our Puritan past. And those who make this criticism do have a point. Christians can fall into the trap of making a big deal of, say, adultery or homosexuality, yet show little concern for the other vices mentioned in these verses, like greed and idolatry. And how does this strike outsiders to the Christian faith? They see it as hypocrisy. In this passage, we see that all of these sins are put on a level playing field at least in this one respect: they are equally damning if they become a pattern of behavior in our lives. Biblical integrity calls us to take sin seriously, not to fixate on the sins we dislike while accommodating others. As Kevin DeYoung writes, "The church should not overlook its other sins just to make homosexual sin seem worse."[2]

I need to mention one last conviction that is at the heart of this passage and the message of this book. *Although we are all sexually broken, we can all become sexually whole through Jesus.* This is the glorious good news about Jesus at the end of these verses. "And that is what some of you were," Paul said to the Corinthians. He's not pointing fingers; he's reminding them of the moral and spiritual pit from which they came. Wouldn't you have loved to see the look on their faces when they heard this! Perhaps they felt a bit embarrassed to have the past brought up? No, not at all. Not in light of what Paul goes on to say: "But you were washed, you were sanctified, you were justified in the name of the Lord Jesus Christ and by the Spirit of our God" (1 Corinthians 6:11).

There is cleansing and healing and forgiveness in Jesus— for all of our sexual brokenness. And if you don't think you are sexually broken, you may be very broken indeed. Sin is pervasive, affecting all of who we are, including our sexuality. And the healing for our sin is found not in ourselves, but in the blood of Jesus.

# BENT SEXUALITY

## JOEL WILLITTS

There should be a sticker with an advisory notice next to the title of this chapter.[1] I'm going to venture into a painful topic, and I'm going to speak about it in a personal way. In doing so, I would like to ask your permission to share with you, in the words of the apostle Paul, "not only the gospel of God but also [my] own [self]" (1 Thessalonians 2:8 ESV). And I would ask for your kindness to me in return, because I am going to put into words elements of my own story that are deeply shameful. I need to name some things that are true but that are very seldom named in church or put in print.

I would also ask you to show kindness to yourself. I may share something in the following pages that stirs you deeply. Be attentive, even kind, to that emotion by blessing it, welcoming it, and honoring it. Let your body speak to you as you perhaps find yourself in my story.

I've titled this essay "Bent Sexuality." I'm grateful to my

friend Todd Wilson for including it in his book on mere sexuality, but if this book is a city you've come to visit for a few days, this chapter will be like crossing over from the gentrified, sparkling part of the city to its seedy underside. But this is an important move to make, because there is more to the story of mere sexuality—the story of those who, like me, follow Jesus with a sense of sexual brokenness, or even bentness.

## The Ambivalence of Sexuality

For me, the mere sexuality that is both biblical and the historic teaching of the church does not sound like a blessing. Instead, I carry it like a *curse in my body*. For me, sexuality feels dark and tainted—a space where God is not. For me, sexuality is not a holy, divine gift. My sexuality is bent. It's warped, and I'm at home there. Strange and twisted as it may sound, this dark sexuality is for me a place of comfort, kindness, and safety. In fact, mere sexuality often feels to me, because of my bent sexuality, like something foreign, awkward, even terrifying.

My sexuality is a burden I have to bear, not a gift I gladly receive. Not long ago, in a moment of clarity, I told my wife, Karla, who has lovingly and patiently walked alongside me on my journey for twenty-three years, "I wish I didn't have a sexuality at all. I wish I didn't have to concern myself with this thing called sexual intimacy. Sex and intimacy are an impossible puzzle for me!" For me, sex is little more than a bodily function that must be performed to regulate stress; everything around it seems chaotic and absurd.

My bent sexuality causes Karla to feel compelled to ask me questions like, "Do you ever desire me sexually?" Vulnerable, honest, searching questions like that from her sink like millstones into my chest. I am filled with self-contempt, fear, confusion, and powerlessness. All I can eke out in terms of a response is not much more than a whispered "I don't know" or "Yes, no." The only thing that is clear is the ambivalence. Even after many hours of therapy, my sexuality is an enigma I feel like I will never crack.

I am a survivor of childhood sexual abuse. My eighteen-year-old stepbrother sexually abused me from age thirteen to sixteen. I'll spare the details here, but this man groomed me into a willing accomplice of his violent perversion. So brilliant a predator was he, I agreeably and enthusiastically became his disciple par excellence and a partner in his sexually warping schemes.

And here's the terrible truth: I'm not alone. Conservative estimates say that about one in four women and one in six men have experienced sexual abuse.[2] These figures woefully underestimate the real situation, however, and this is particularly true for men. Since nearly 90 percent of sexual predators are men, sexually abused men have increased levels of shame resulting from same-sex sexual contact that results in far less self-reporting in the types of paper-pencil surveys that produce these figures.

In addition, most of us don't really know what constitutes sexual abuse in the first place. If I asked you, "How would you define sexual abuse?" how would you answer the question? You surely would think a story like mine fits any definition. But it took me several years before I ever thought to name what had happened to me "abuse." This is because I felt I had "enjoyed" and "participated in" the sexual relationship. How could it be abuse if I was joining in *willfully*, if I was the sidekick in this deceptive, dark scheme in the family? However, I had never considered the power dynamic that is always at work in abuse.

The first time I ever named my abuse to anyone was during my sophomore year in college, while serving on a summer counseling staff at a Christian camp. One of my campers late one night shared that he had been molested by a youth worker. For the first time, I saw myself in his story.

## Defining Sexual Abuse

When we understand what exactly sexual abuse is, we will find that more of us have been affected by abuse than we have ever realized. I've taken over this definition of sexual abuse (SA) from Christian therapist Dr. Dan Allender: "SA is a sexual experience initiated by a person of power (usually older) with a person who is not in a position to refuse (usually younger)."[3]

The anatomy of abuse, then, involves two components: (1) an invitation to a sexual experience of any kind, and (2) an unequal power dynamic such that the victim cannot imagine refusing.

On this understanding, many things we take for granted in our hypersexualized culture are, in fact, sexual abuse. Take, for instance, an older boy introducing a younger boy to pornography. While this is regularly viewed as "boys being boys," it is, in fact, an act of abuse and has, as attested by many men with whom I have spoken, tremendous negative impact on a person's sexuality. Often this early introduction to sexuality creates a wound they forever carry around in their body.

Another recent example comes from the arena of NCAA Division 1 collegiate sports. In the fall of 2015, a sex scandal erupted involving the University of Louisville's basketball team when a former escort, Katina Powell, admitted in an exposé that she organized nearly two dozen stripping and sex parties from 2010 to 2014 inside Billy Minardi Hall, the on-campus dorm for athletes. The parties were set up during recruitment visits. ESPN's *Outside the Lines* interviewed five former players, one of whom said he attended these parties. One of these players admitted having sex after a graduate assistant paid for it. Another said, "I knew they weren't college girls. It was crazy. It was like I was in a strip club."[4] The details of this scandal possess the two elements of sexual abuse: the invitation into a sexual encounter and an uneven power dynamic. It is hard to imagine a potential recruit having the maturity or courage to excuse himself from this sort of thing.

The subsequent sports talk—the main subject of so many in the week following—was disconcerting, as many male sports radio hosts had little problem with the sexual exploitation of women and the sexual abuse of young men and seemed only to care about what the scandal meant for the already embattled future Hall of Fame coach Rick Pitino. This episode reveals just how little our macho, sports-saturated North American culture understands its role in perpetuating sexual abuse and how little we still understand about its nature, in spite of publicized cases like the Penn State Jerry Sandusky case.

## The Aftermath of Sexual Abuse

What happens to a person who has been sexually abused? We can use a variety of categories to answer this question. I want to point out two very important categories of aftermath.

The first is *survival* by any and every means. In his book *The Healing Path*, Dan Allender describes four paths survivors take in the aftermath of sexual trauma, all of which are ways that lead away from healing. Survivors may be:

1. Paranoid ("Life is difficult, then you die").
2. Fatalistic ("Qué será, será—roll with it, baby").
3. Heroic ("What does not kill me makes me stronger").
4. Optimistic ("Just grin and bear it").[5]

All four of these have in common the avoidance of pain. This intentionality to avoid pain has all kinds of negative effects. One of the most significant is the way these approaches "take the person out" emotionally in intimate interpersonal moments. Survivors share the struggle to stay present and often are perceived as aloof and difficult to know because of their hypervigilance in protecting themselves from further pain. Allender writes:

> The paranoiac avoids pain by seeing it everywhere and with everyone. He avoids disappointment by never being surprised by sorrow. The fatalist avoids pain by accepting it as normal and part of the impersonal "luck" of life. The hero avoids it by seizing it as an opportunity to grow without ever acknowledging need or weakness. The optimist avoids pain by seeing all the good surrounding it in other areas of life.[6]

The problem is, the only route to healing winds its way through treacherous passes of the grief of our wounds. Our pain is an invitation to grieve what evil has done and is doing, and naming it with an empathetic and skilled loved one is the path to restoration.

But if we boil it down, victims of sexual abuse survive. And they survive by any and all means. Most often, though, survival strategies perpetuate the sexual dysfunction initiated by the predator, even if the abuser is well out of the picture, as in my case.

The second category is *bodily injury*. Survivors have been injured bodily, some of it at times visible, but much of it hidden in the brain. Brain science, regularly referred to as neuroscience or neuropsychology, is teaching us that trauma leaves bodily injury deep in the structures of the brain. Trauma, in fact, changes the *physiology* of the brain. In trauma, neuron pathways are created that affect the way we respond to stimuli. Neurons are electrical messengers in our brain that control unconscious responses. *Neuroplasticity* is the term used to refer to the way neurons create neural networks in our brain for easy travel between domains of our brain that generate responses and patterns of thought.[7] Our brains have been literally shaped by traumatic experiences, and these patterns exert an influence on our bodies at a level below our consciousness. I've heard Dan Allender say, "Our neurons remember," even if we don't.[8] Christian therapist Joy Schroeder writes, "Memories of sexual abuse can be integrally bound up with the body. Some victims have visible scars, permanent injuries, chronic pains, sexually transmitted diseases, and pregnancy. For others, the scars are not visible, but memory of the abuse remains lodged in the psyche and as body memory.[9]

In his very important book *Our Bodies Keep Score*, Bessel van der Kolk explains something that could very well revolutionize how we approach spiritual formation when it comes to bent sexuality. He notes that the advances in neurological science "help us understand why traumatized people so often keep repeating the same problems and have such trouble learning from experience. We now know that their behaviors are not the result of moral failings or signs of lack of will-power or bad character—they are caused by actual changes in the brain."[10]

I know of few approaches to spiritual formation within the evangelical church subculture that adequately account for our bodies in the process of spiritual transformation.[11] I know of few that have understood the physiology of sexual brokenness and taken it sufficiently into account in Christian formation.

Now add to this ecclesial deficiency the fact that many people either don't remember or don't recognize their own trauma around sexuality because of the tendency to minimize its impact ("It wasn't that bad") or to repress the memories ("I've never been abused"). Minimization and dissociation are the two most common strategies employed by a survivor of abuse.

In sum, left to themselves, survivors of sexual abuse are sexually dysfunctional, wounded internally, and unable to fully express emotions in a healthy way. They fear and avoid intimacy and are hypervigilant in relationships. Often they either lack sexual desire completely or are hypersexual. And they have hidden bodily wounds that are no less severe than if they had lost a hand or a foot. Furthermore, tragically many are walking around in quiet shame and despair because they are sexually bent and unaware of their own story.

## Sexual Abuse and Mere Sexuality

It is clear that sexual abuse significantly problematizes any attempt to simplify sexuality and Christian spiritual formation. And this is true for a greater number of people in our churches than we realize. So when I hear a sermon on sexuality—and I've heard my fair share—I usually don't feel the preacher has fully considered the implications of sexual abuse, even if he made an occasional mention of sexual brokenness.

For example, many men who preach about sexuality assume things about male sexual desire that little reflect my own experience. My struggle, for example, is not with a wild, uncontrollable sexual desire, but with the opposite, namely, the absence of sexual desire and a desire to avoid it. For me, sexual desire always feels like a dark desire. While created good and holy by God—I take this on faith in the teaching of both the Bible and the church—my sexual desire only seems to me a dark, unholy thing.

So a Christian teacher can announce to me the truth about sexuality, but my body tells me something very different; and because of where this knowledge resides, it is not something I can simply reprogram cognitively. Simply memorizing the logic of a spiritual equation like $2 + 2 = 4$ does not "fix" it for me, because when I work out the equation in my logic, I always come out with 5, not 4. There is, quite literally, a short circuit in my neuron pathway. This is not a software problem; it's a hardware problem. My sexual bentness is in my bones, so to speak, not merely in my mind.

So the remedies for sexual sin and brokenness that spiritual leaders offer me have only ever given me short-lived management strategies, never real, lasting freedom. When I read the boldly asserted promise of wholeness from sexual brokenness in Jesus like that offered in Todd's first chapter, I'll be honest—I fight cynicism because I know how hard I have tried. After three decades of white-knuckle fighting, I continue to fail to curb my disoriented sexuality. And I feel the cold shadow of the Evil One as he whispers words of accusation, contempt, and shame into my ear: "You are just not disciplined enough. You are not surrendered enough. You don't love God enough. You are not enough. You have to work harder." I just want to scream, "To hell with it! Forget it all!"

I believe such preachers and writers are well-meaning. But they can, inadvertently, do more harm than good, at least to some. The preacher who essentially offers something like "memorize two verses and call me in the morning" as the means of healing or overcoming sexual sin has not begun to grasp the complexity of sexuality and the irreducible connection between our body and our spiritual person.

Do I believe healing, wholeness, and restoration are both possible and available? Yes, I do. But most often the healing comes in fits and starts. It is the result of a long, painful process, and in all likelihood it will not be completed until Jesus returns. Why? Because our bodies continue to be made of the stuff of the earth—stuff that is still awaiting restoration (see Romans 8:22–23). The apostle Paul captures this long view when he points to the restoration of our bodies as a consequence of the second coming of Jesus. On that day Christ will, Paul says, "transform our lowly bodies so that they will be like his glorious body" (Philippians 3:21).

## The Hopeful Realism of Mere Sexuality

In what follows, I offer a hopeful realism for those of us who are sexually bent. I hope to do three things: (1) to thicken the description of mere sexuality by taking into account evil's all-out assault on our sexuality and particularly on our sexual desires; (2) to invite us to step courageously into the places of our sexual shame, because that is where we will encounter Jesus, who has come to speak God's word of kindness and to defend us before the Evil One; and (3) to transform our perspective of broken and bent sexuality from a story of contempt to a story of kindness.

## Sexual Bentness Meets Mere Sexuality

I have found the story of Jesus' encounter with a woman caught in adultery in John 8 to be a story with life-giving truth for those who are sexually bent. This is a story of what happens when a sexually bent woman meets the embodiment of mere sexuality, Jesus.

The author tells the story in seven movements. You may want to open a Bible to John 8:1–11 as you review these narrative stages:[12]

1. The scribes and Pharisees brought a woman to Jesus who had been "caught in adultery" and asked him a question about Jewish law (verses 2–5).

2. The narrator interrupts and states their motive: to test Jesus so they might accuse him (verse 6a).

3. Jesus stooped down and wrote on the ground with his finger (verse 6b).

4. The scribes and Pharisees persisted, and Jesus stood up and said, "Let any one of you who is without sin be the first to throw a stone at her." Then he stooped down again and continued to write (verses 7–8).

5. The scribes and Pharisees, one by one, dropped their stones and left the scene, beginning with the oldest among them. Jesus and the woman were left alone (verse 9).

6. Jesus asked the woman where her accusers were; she responded that none remained (verses 10–11a).

7. Jesus told her he didn't condemn her and told her to go and sin no more (verse 11b).

Let's think about this story through its characters.

**The Narrator.** The narrator is not properly a character in the story, but his role is perhaps the most important because he gives us an omniscient perspective on the story. What do we learn from the authorial insertion in John 8:6a? The author wants us to see that behind this story is another story. The narrator unmasks the Evil One behind this story. The woman is not the central character in this drama, as it turns out. In fact, referring to this story as "The Woman Caught in Adultery" is to miss the main point. The Evil One's purposes are not focused on her. She is but a pawn in a match between the forces of evil and God. "The scribes and the Pharisees" are the embodiment of evil's intentions against God. Their intention is to bring an accusation, not against this woman merely, but against the Son of God. This is a crucial biblical perspective we need to grasp. In scholarly speak, this is called "apocalypticism." One scholar has called it "the mother of New Testament theology."[13] The war in the heavenly realm, while won through Christ's death and resurrection, is still being fought in the trenches of our day-to-day lives until Jesus returns. The Evil One is fighting God's using us, and he is attacking us at the core of our identity, namely, our sexuality.

**The Evil One.** The author wants us to see that behind this whole scenario is the Evil One. He continues to this day to assault God's image bearers just as he did in the garden (Genesis 3:1–3), seeking to harm them at the point where he can do the most damage: their ability to give and receive love. M. Scott Peck usefully describes evil as an attempt to kill, as "opposition to life," as "killing that is not required for biological survival."[14] Evil is also that which kills the spirit and any element of the attributes of human life. "Evil . . . is that force, residing either inside or outside of human beings, that seeks to kill life or liveliness."[15] This is the work of the Evil One in this story and in our own.

In the story's details, we can see both the Evil One's common strategy of abuse and the inevitable outcome of his assault. As with almost every sexually abusive encounter, the perpetrator follows a clear strategy involving (1) the setup of the victim (John 8:3), (2) the utility of the victim (verse 6), and then (3) the victim's disposal (verse 5). The victim is preyed on and then thrown away.

The outcome is dehumanization, the inability to be fully human. The Evil One takes away the capacity to be God's image bearer. The victim is rendered incapable both of having a healthy view of himself or herself and of having intimate relationships with others and with God. The victim instead diminishes as a human being through shame and contempt (disdain) for self and others. A victim of abuse feels shame for a host of reasons, some obvious and others not so obvious. The shame produced by the abuse is the Evil One's greatest weapon. It renders the victim powerless, betrayed, and in a state of silent ambivalence.

**The Victim.** The woman is an adulteress, but she is also clearly a victim of abuse. And the two states are interrelated—the latter being the consequence of the former. We must not miss that connection. Abuse is anything that involves exploitation of a weaker person by a stronger, more powerful person. Of course, the mistreatment doesn't have to be physically violent to be violent. Every type of abuse is violence. Abuse is an assault on our personhood. This woman had experienced the violence of a male-dominated society. Given her cultural position, it would be difficult to isolate and identify where she may have had any clear choices in this whole affair. She was no match for the powers at work around her. If we put ourselves in the shoes of a woman in antiquity, we may find an empathy for her that many Christians miss when reading the story. Did she really have resources to make different choices? Did she make the choices that seemed best to her to survive? Since she is in the midst of a circle with Jesus at the center, the author seems to invite us to have empathy for her.

Furthermore, while the story does not divulge the answer, we should ask what series of events brought her to this place. We see the end of the story—her adultery—but what was the beginning or the middle? Where along the line did she ally with the Evil One to choose the adulterous path? Would she even have had the resources to do otherwise? What strategies of survival might she have come to rely on that in the end only led to more shame, more vulnerability, more pain? By the way, you don't just end up an adulteress. She is one, but she is more than that. As is always the case, there is both a depravity to be grieved and a dignity to be admired.

Jesus will not excuse her sexual misconduct, to be sure. But at the same time, it is clear from the story that for him, her sexual sin is not the primary issue.

## The Eternal Word of God to the Sexually Bent

Jesus silenced her accusers with playful strength. We will never know what he wrote in the dirt. But in any case, the action underscored Jesus' identity as the most powerful person in the story. In his action, Jesus released the woman from the power of shame reflected in the eyes of her accusers. Furthermore, Jesus empowered her to *rewrite her story.* He invited her into a new kind of life—one oriented and motivated by the kindness of God, one that empowered her to imagine life beyond sexual bentness.

"Neither do I condemn you; go, and from now on sin no more" (John 8:11 ESV). These were Jesus' only words to her in the scene, but these words forever defined her. This was Jesus' word to her there and ever thereafter. This is Jesus' word to the sexually bent—not just the first word, but his eternal word. "Neither do I condemn you; go, and from now on sin no more" is the eternal word of Jesus to us.

## The Complexity of Sexual Sin and the Path toward Restoration

Interestingly, Jesus' statement to the woman reveals the complex nature of sexual sin and offers a guide toward sexual restoration. Every sexual sin involves two factors that must be understood, distinguished, named, confessed, and grieved in the midst of loving, Spirit-filled, and skilled listeners.

**The initial wound.** First, the origin of every sexual sin is an assault by the Evil One. At the point of origin of every deviant sexual behavior is a *wound.* In my experience in the church, this is the least recognized but most important aspect of redemption. If we are ever to be redeemed, we must hear the first word of kindness: "Neither do I condemn you." *It* *was not your fault!* The original sexual deviant act was not done by you; it was done to you. *You were just a young boy. What did you know? How could you have ever seen it coming? You so desired to be noticed. You were so adventurous. Where were your protectors? Who should have defended you? You were no match for what you were invited into.* This "original sin" must be named and grieved. We must hold the brokenness, the abandonment, and the exploitation. If we are to know the utter goodness of redemption, we must name the bitter truth about our lives: "I am a victim of sexual abuse." The pattern of a deviant sexuality is the aftermath of our wound. We must begin with the compassion of Jesus to release the young boy or girl from culpability. It was not her fault: "Neither do I condemn you."

**Alliance with evil.** An important second factor must be dealt with as well. Each of us, as a result of our intitial wound, has consciously or unconsciously made a vow to protect ourselves from harm and from the pain of the truth. I have come to see in my own life that one such vow has been a declaration that I will never again trust another person. This was not a conscious decision, but as I read my own story, I see this as a clear pattern in my life. I live independently of others. I look to no one for comfort. This vow, however effective it has been at protecting my heart, renders me incapable of experiencing the fullness of life. What's more, it imprisons me in a bent sexuality. I'm living fragmentedly and as half a person, and I'm weighed down by the shame of a bent sexuality.

What's more, this vow making and the pattern of life that

flows from it mean we have allied with the Evil One against ourselves and others. This may sound unkind at first, but it is true: victims of abuse end up wounding themselves and others to a far greater degree than the initial wound. While as survivors we should never feel compelled to repent of the sin committed against us, we must come to a point of repenting of the sins we have perpetrated on others in our attempts to survive. This, I think, is what Jesus' "go, and from now on sin no more" means. Unless we deal with both of these factors, we unintentionally cut ourselves off from God's healing, restorative grace.

## Conclusion

In conclusion, let me say something to two groups of people. First, *to the church*. The move away from what we've called "mere sexuality" is not *only* the result of a cultural shift in views on sexuality in the post–sexual revolutionary world. The church itself must take ownership of its failure to provide a compelling vision of sexuality historically. The church, for many historical reasons—the influence of Neoplatonism and the rejection of the body, to name one major factor—has abrogated influence on sexuality. Additionally, rampant sexual abuse is not a modern phenomenon; it's as ancient as time.

Sexuality that falls short of mere sexuality is often connected to abuse. A legion of disciples of Jesus are struggling to follow Jesus with a sense of bentness. The church needs to take Jesus' approach. We need to speak his word of kindness and life. We must invite people to honesty, to naming the harm the Evil One has done and expressing their grief. I believe that is the gift of the practice of lament, and I'm convinced that the human body must have a much greater place in our program of discipleship.

The second word is *to the survivor*. In his novel *Remembering*, Wendell Berry tells the story of Andy, who lost his hand in a farming accident.[16] Much of the story is about the disorienting struggle to live without his right hand. Berry's imaginative prose captures the disordered bodily world of a trauma survivor. While invisible for most, the injury of sexual abuse is not less bodily than the loss of a limb. As Andy's body is altered by the accident, so too were mine and yours altered by sexual abuse. And while God can do anything and he may restore fully in this age, it is also true that we may carry our sexual wounds to the resurrection. In our bent sexuality, we need to hear again and again Jesus' eternal word: "Neither do I condemn you; go, and from now on sin no more."

You may have experienced a deep trauma over which you had no choice and for which you have no fault. You didn't put yourself in harm's way. Jesus invites us into a place of God's kindness and presence. He engages our hearts tenderly, empathetically, kindly. He is with us, protecting us from the Evil One. He speaks prophetically, opening up the prospect of a different kind of life, if we will take the risk. He is inviting us into the newness of life through repentance. Paul writes in Romans 2:4, "God's kindness is intended to lead you to repentance," not to his contempt. If you are weary of the fight, if you are tired of white-knuckling it through your bent sexuality, know that Jesus offers a different path. I invite you onto his path through trust in his kindness and through repentance of your independence.

# ACKNOWLEDGMENTS

I acknowledge with gratitude and joy those who have helped me with this book. Pride of place goes to my church family. This book began life as a sermon series preached at Calvary Memorial Church in Oak Park, Illinois, where I have had the privilege of serving as pastor for nearly a decade. Their receptivity to the series and thoughtful interaction with its content enriched my own thinking considerably. To the elders, ministry staff, and congregation, I am deeply indebted.

A number of people read earlier drafts of this book and offered feedback: Rae Wilson, Beth and Mike Jones, Andy Isch, John Isch, Ted Griffin, Randal Hess, Drew Carter, Soo Ai Kudo, Steve Williamson, Chris Bruno, Max Clayton, Matthew Mason, Bill Suriano, Preston Sprinkle, Matthew Lee Anderson, Steve Wilson, Greg Enas, and Harry Parker. I'm grateful to them for giving their time and sharing their insights to help improve this book. I would also like to thank my friend Joel Willitts, who was kind and courageous enough to share his own story with our church family and then in this book.

The team at Zondervan has, as always, been a delight to work with, especially Ryan Pazdur, Nathan Kroeze, and Dirk Buursma. I owe a very special thanks to Ryan, who cheerfully took on this project and skillfully shepherded it to publication.

As always, my wife, Katie, has been a steady source of wisdom, encouragement, and support. Her love for books, ideas, people, and, most importantly, Jesus Christ has enriched not only this project but my life—and that in countless ways.

Finally, I've dedicated this book to Wesley Hill. We first met nearly twenty years ago while Wesley was still a high school student, and I a recent college grad. Our friendship blossomed, though, when we overlapped for a season at Wheaton College, Wesley working on a BA, and I on an MA. Weekly sessions in the Stupe forged a bond that endures to this day. I greatly admire Wesley for not only his brilliant mind and generous heart but his sterling example of fidelity to his Lord and mine—Jesus Christ. Wesley truly is an ἐπιστολὴ Χριστοῦ.

*Soli Deo Gloria!*

# NOTES

## Introduction

1. Representative examples would be Kevin DeYoung, *What Does the Bible Really Teach about Homosexuality?* (Wheaton, IL: Crossway, 2015), and Chad Thompson, *Loving Homosexuals as Jesus Would: A Fresh Christian Approach* (Grand Rapids: Brazos, 2004).

2. For example, DeYoung, *What Does the Bible Really Teach about Homosexuality?*; Preston Sprinkle, *People to Be Loved: Why Homosexuality Is Not Just an Issue* (Grand Rapids: Zondervan, 2015); Robert Gagnon, *The Bible and Homosexual Practice: Texts and Hermeneutics* (Nashville: Abingdon, 2002); and from an affirming perspective, James V. Brownson, *Bible, Gender, Sexuality: Reframing the Church's Debate on Same-Sex Relationships* (Grand Rapids: Eerdmans, 2013).

3. I'm indebted to Mark A. Yarhouse, *Homosexuality and the Christian* (Minneapolis: Bethany House, 2010), 158, for the

categories "sincere struggler" and "assertive advocate." The other three categories are my own.

4. Justin Lee, *Torn: Rescuing the Gospel from the Gays-vs.-Christians Debate* (New York: Jericho, 2012); Matthew Vines, *God and the Gay Christian: The Biblical Case in Support of Same-Sex Relationships* (New York: Convergent, 2014).

5. Oliver O'Donovan, *Church in Crisis: The Gay Controversy and the Anglican Communion* (Eugene, OR: Cascade, 2008), 108.

6. See Wesley Hill, "Once More: On the Label 'Gay Christian,'" *First Things*, February 1, 2013, www.firstthings.com/blogs/firstthoughts/2013/02/once-more-on-the-label-gay-christian (accessed February 10, 2017).

7. Preston Sprinkle gets it right: "I don't think it is necessarily wrong to describe yourself as 'gay,' if you are using the term not to speak of your core identity but your unique experience as a same-sex attracted person" (*People to Be Loved*, 142).

8. Sam Allberry, *Is God Anti-Gay? And Other Questions about Homosexuality, the Bible and Same-Sex Attraction*, rev. ed. (Epsom, Surrey, UK: Good Book Company, 2015), 10–11, emphasis original.

9. Wesley Hill, *Washed and Waiting: Reflections on Christian Faithfulness & Homosexuality*, rev. ed. (2010; repr., Grand Rapids: Zondervan, 2016), 22.

## Chapter 1: What Is Mere Sexuality

1. Quoted in Michael Paulson, "With Same-Sex Decision, Evangelical Churches Address New Reality," *New York*

*Times*, June 28, 2015, www.nytimes.com/2015/06/29/us/with-same-sex-decision-evangelical-churches-address-new-reality.html?_r=0 (accessed February 10, 2017).

2. See Kate Tracy, "Wheaton Students Protest 'Train Wreck Conversion' Speaker's Ex-Gay Testimony," *Christianity Today*, February 21, 2014, www.christianitytoday.com/gleanings/2014/february/wheaton-students-protest-exgay-chapel-rosaria-butterfield.html (accessed February 10, 2017).

3. Quoted in Gayla R. Postma, "Wolterstorff: Biblical Justice and Same-Sex Marriage," *Banner*, October 24, 2016, http://thebanner.org/news/2016/10/wolterstorff-biblical-justice-and-same-sex-marriage (accessed February 10, 2017). For critical interaction with Wolterstorff, see Matthew Tuininga, "Sexuality and the Gospel: My Response to Nicholas Wolterstorff," *Perspectives: A Journal of Reformed Thought*, December 4, 2016, https://perspectivesjournal.org/blog/2016/12/04/sexuality-gospel-response-nicholas-wolterstorff (accessed February 10, 2017)—though see Nicholas Wolterstorff, "Response to Matthew Tuininga on Sexuality and Scripture," *Perspectives*, December 4, 2016, https://perspectivesjournal.org/blog/2016/12/04/response-matthew-tuininga-sexuality-scripture/?preview_id=10436 (accessed February 10, 2017); see esp. Wesley Hill, "Nicholas Wolterstorff's Cheap Shots," *First Things*, November 1, 2016, www.firstthings.com/web-exclusives/2016/11/nicholas-wolterstorffs-cheap-shots (accessed February 10, 2017).

4. Glennon Doyle Melton, *Love Warrior: A Memoir* (New York: Macmillan, 2016).

5. Quoted in Kate Shellnutt, "A Christian Mom Blogger Announces She's Dating Soccer Star Abby Wambach," *Washington Post*, November 14, 2016, www.washingtonpost .com/news/acts-of-faith/wp/2016/11/14/a-christian -mom-blogger-announces-shes-dating-soccer-star-abby -wambach/?utm_term=.72e0a24140b1 (accessed February 10, 2017).

6. See Pew Research Center, "Changing Attitudes on Gay Marriage: Public Opinion on Same-Sex Marriage," May 12, 2016, www.pewforum.org/2016/05/12/changing -attitudes-on-gay-marriage (accessed February 10, 2017).

7. See Justin Lee, *Torn: Rescuing the Gospel from the Gays-vs.-Christians Debate* (New York: Jericho, 2012), chapter 2, "God Boy"; similarly, Matthew Vines, *God and the Gay Christian: The Biblical Case in Support of Same-Sex Relationships* (New York: Convergent, 2014).

8. See Robert D. Putnam and David E. Campbell, *American Grace: How Religion Divides and Unites Us* (New York: Simon & Schuster, 2010), 127–29, 402–6.

9. Christian Smith, *The Bible Made Impossible: Why Biblicism Is Not a Truly Evangelical Reading of Scripture* (Grand Rapids: Brazos, 2011), 3, 17. I should note that one need not come to all the same conclusions as Smith to grant the saliency of his point about the problem of pervasive interpretive pluralism.

10. Jen Hatmaker, "World Vision, Gay Marriage, and a Different Way Through," March 25, 2014, http://

jenhatmaker.com/blog/2014/03/25/world-vision-gay
-marriage-and-a-different-way-through (accessed
February 10, 2017), emphasis original.

11. For a fascinating discussion of the origins of morality and
moral intuition, see Jonathan Haidt, *The Righteous Mind:
Why Good People Are Divided by Politics and Religion* (New
York: Vintage, 2013), 3–31.

12. Karl Barth, *Church Dogmatics: The Doctrine of Creation*,
volume 3, part 4 (New York: T&T Clark, 1961), 166. I'm
indebted to Christopher C. Roberts for alerting me to this
reference (*Creation & Covenant: The Significance of Sexual
Difference in the Moral Theology of Marriage* [New York:
Bloomsbury Academic, 2007], 161).

13. See Peter L. Berger and Thomas Luckmann, *The Social
Construction of Reality: A Treatise in the Sociology of Knowledge*
(New York: Penguin, 1966), esp. 154–70.

14. Ross Douthat, *Bad Religion: How We Became a Nation of
Heretics* (New York: Free Press, 2013), 70.

15. Luke Timothy Johnson, "Homosexuality & the Church,"
*Commonweal*, June 11, 2007, www.commonwealmagazine
.org/homosexuality-church-1 (accessed February 10, 2017).

16. I want to thank Matthew Mason, rector of Christ Church
Salisbury (UK), for pointing out this terminological
distinction.

17. In his carefully researched book on the significance of
sexual difference for the moral theology of marriage,
Christopher C. Roberts shows that for centuries, there
has been a Christian consensus on sexuality. He explains:
"After an initial patristic period in which Christian beliefs

about sexual difference were fluctuating and diverse, a more or less rough consensus on sexual difference existed from the fourth to the twentieth centuries" (*Creation & Covenant*, 185–86). He summarizes: "There is an ancient Christian tradition, from Augustine to John Paul II, which has believed and argued that sexual difference is significant" (236).

18. See Alasdair MacIntyre, *After Virtue: A Study in Moral Theory*, 3rd ed. (New York: Bloomsbury, 2007), 257.

19. Consider the assessment of German theologian Wolfhart Pannenberg: "If a church were to let itself be pushed to the point where it ceased to treat homosexual activity as a departure from the biblical norm, and recognized homosexual unions as a personal partnership of love equivalent to marriage, such a church would stand no longer on biblical ground but against the unequivocal witness of Scripture. A church that took this step would cease to be the one, holy, catholic, and apostolic church" ("Revelation and Homosexual Experience," *Christianity Today*, November 11, 1996, www.christianitytoday.com/ct/1996/november11/6td035.html [accessed February 10, 2017]).

20. Kyle Harper, *From Shame to Sin: The Christian Transformation of Sexual Morality in Late Antiquity* (Cambridge, MA: Harvard University Press, 2013), 3.

## Chapter 2: The Sexuality of Jesus

1. On the importance of grounding anthropology in Christology and of reckoning with the fact that not only is Jesus human but he also reveals true humanity,

see Marc Cortez, *Christological Anthropology in Historical Perspective: Ancient and Contemporary Approaches to Theological Anthropology* (Grand Rapids: Zondervan, 2016), 17–29. Of relevance to this chapter is Cortez's fascinating discussion of Gregory of Nyssa's transformative Christology and its implications for his conception of human sexuality (31–55).

2. On the necessity of establishing Christian ethics on evangelical foundations, see chapter 1 in Oliver O'Donovan, *Resurrection and Moral Order: An Outline for Evangelical Ethics* (Grand Rapids: Eerdmans, 1986), 11–27. As O'Donovan warns, "There can be ethical Christians without there being Christian ethics" (11).

3. Mark D. Regnerus, *Forbidden Fruit: Sex & Religion in the Lives of American Teenagers* (New York: Oxford University Press, 2007), 214.

4. See David Kinnaman and Gabe Lyons, *unChristian: What a New Generation Really Thinks about Christianity . . . and Why It Matters* (Grand Rapids: Baker, 2007).

5. See Phil Zuckerman, *Faith No More: Why People Reject Religion* (New York: Oxford University Press, 2012), 74–87.

6. Preston Sprinkle, *People to Be Loved: Why Homosexuality Is Not Just an Issue* (Grand Rapids: Zondervan, 2015), 69.

7. Debra Hirsh, *Redeeming Sex: Naked Conversations about Sexuality and Spirituality* (Downers Grove, IL: InterVarsity, 2015), 50.

8. So Harold O. J. Brown, *Heresies: The Image of Christ in the Mirror of Heresy and Orthodoxy from the Apostles to the Present* (Garden City, NY: Doubleday, 1984), 30.

9. Westminster Confession of Faith, chapter 8, article 2, in Philip Schaff, *The Evangelical Protestant Creeds*, vol. 3 of *The Creeds of Christendom* (Grand Rapids: Baker, 1983), 619.

10. Donald Macleod, *The Person of Christ* (Downers Grove, IL: InterVarsity, 1998), 162.

11. Ibid.

12. Walter Moberly, "The Use of Scripture in Contemporary Debate about Homosexuality," *Theology* 103 (July–August 2000): 254, http://journals.sagepub.com/doi/pdf/10.1177/0040571X0010300403 (accessed February 10, 2017).

13. Caitlyn Jenner, "My Story: Finally Free!" http://caitlynjenner.com/my-story (accessed February 10, 2017).

14. Quoted in Amanda Petrusich, "Free to Be Miley," *Paper* magazine, June 9, 2015.

15. Richard B. Hays, *The Moral Vision of the New Testament: A Contemporary Introduction to New Testament Ethics* (San Francisco: HarperSanFrancisco, 1996), 401.

16. Justin Lee, *Torn: Rescuing the Gospel from the Gays-vs.-Christians Debate* (New York: Jericho, 2012), 103.

17. Ibid.

18. See Kevin DeYoung, *What Does the Bible Really Teach about Homosexuality?* (Wheaton, IL: Crossway, 2015); Preston Sprinkle, *People to Be Loved: Why Homosexuality Is Not Just an Issue* (Grand Rapids: Zondervan, 2015); Robert Gagnon, *The Bible and Homosexual Practice: Texts and Hermeneutics* (Nashville: Abingdon, 2002).

19. C. S. Lewis, *Mere Christianity* (1943; repr., New York: Macmillan, 1960), 124–25.

20. Wesley Hill, *Washed and Waiting: Reflections on Christian Faithfulness & Homosexuality*, rev. ed. (2010; repr., Grand Rapids: Zondervan, 2016), 76, emphasis original.
21. Ibid., 84.
22. Ibid., 111.
23. Ibid., 112.

## Chapter 3: Male, Female, and the *Imago Dei*

1. See David Cohen, "Not Just Male and Female Anymore: Facebook Introduces Custom Genders," *Adweek*, February 13, 2014, www.adweek.com/digital/custom-genders (accessed February 10, 2017).
2. Ibid.
3. "Germany Allows 'Indeterminate' Gender at Birth," *BBC News*, November 1, 2013, video interview, www.bbc.com/news/world-europe-24767225 (accessed February 10, 2017).
4. Jenell Williams Paris, *The End of Sexual Identity: Why Sex Is Too Important to Define Who We Are* (Downers Grove, IL: InterVarsity, 2011), 41.
5. Ibid.
6. See the incisive analysis in Rosaria Champagne Butterfield, *Openness Unhindered: Further Thoughts of an Unlikely Convert on Sexual Identity and Union with Christ* (Pittsburgh, PA: Crown & Covenant, 2015), 93–112.
7. Avery Wallace, "Opinion: 'It's a Girl!' Not So Fast . . . ," *CNN*, March 19, 2015, www.cnn.com/2015/03/17/opinions/avery-wallace-teen (accessed February 10, 2017).

8. Oliver O'Donovan, *Church in Crisis: The Gay Controversy and the Anglican Communion* (Eugene, OR: Cascade, 2008), 112. More sober reflection, however, suggests otherwise. As O'Donovan writes, "Sexual desire in particular is notoriously difficult to interpret."

9. Butterfield, *Openness Unhindered*, 6, emphasis original; see also chapters 4–5, where she describes the nineteenth-century advent of the notion of "sexual orientation" and with it the transformation of personal identity.

10. Scholarly discussion of the image of God is vast. For a helpful assessment, see John F. Kilner, *Dignity and Destiny: Humanity in the Image of God* (Grand Rapids: Eerdmans, 2015).

11. Karl Barth, *Church Dogmatics: The Doctrine of Creation*, volume 3, part 2 (New York: T&T Clark, 1961), 324 (cited in Christopher C. Roberts, *Creation & Covenant* [New York: Bloomsbury Academic, 2007], 142).

12. I'm indebted to Barth's development of this framework of "male or female" and "male and female" in his *Church Dogmatics* (volume 3, part 4, 116–240).

13. I'm aware of the challenge to the male-female sexual binary posed by the unique medical condition known as intersex, yet I remain unconvinced. See Megan K. DeFranza, *Sex Difference in Christian Theology: Male, Female, and Intersex in the Image of God* (Grand Rapids: Eerdmans, 2015). While I disagree with her main contention and some of her conclusions, she has provided the church a helpful service by reflecting so substantively and sensitively on the reality of intersex persons. Not

unrelated is the experience known as "gender dysphoria," which is helpfully discussed by Mark Yarhouse, *Gender Dysphoria: Navigating Transgender Issues in a Changing Culture* (Downers Grove, IL: InterVarsity, 2015).

14. Melinda Selmys, *Sexual Authenticity: An Intimate Reflection on Homosexuality and Catholicism* (Huntington, IN: Our Sunday Visitor, 2009), 209.

15. Barth, *Church Dogmatics*, volume 3, part 4, 163.

16. For helpful reflections on the significance of gender difference, see Sam A. Andreades, *enGendered: God's Gift of Gender Difference in Relationship* (Wooster, OH: Weaver, 2015).

17. J. Budziszewski, *On the Meaning of Sex* (Wilmington, DE: ISI, 2012), 61.

## Chapter 4: "One Flesh"

1. See Aaron Morrison, "Will Supreme Court Gay Marriage Ruling End Culture Wars? Activists on Both Sides Say No," *International Business Times*, June 26, 2015, www .ibtimes.com/will-supreme-court-gay-marriage-ruling -end-culture-wars-activists-both-sides-say-no-1974987 (accessed February 10, 2017).

2. See Sherif Girgis, Ryan T. Anderson, and Robert P. George, *What Is Marriage? Man and Woman: A Defense* (New York: Encounter, 2012); Patrick Lee and Robert P. George, *Conjugal Union: What Marriage Is and Why It Matters* (Cambridge: Cambridge University Press, 2014).

3. See Kate Shellnutt, "I Didn't Marry My Best Friend:

Couples Need More Than Just Each Other," *Christianity Today*, September 15, 2014, www.christianitytoday.com/ct/2014/september/i-didnt-marry-my-best-friend.html (accessed February 10, 2017).

4. While the primary emphasis of the phrase "one flesh" in Genesis 2:24 may not be sexual but familial—or as affirming scholar James V. Brownson says, "a lifelong *kinship* bond" (*Bible, Gender, Sexuality: Reframing the Church's Debate on Same-Sex Relationships* [Grand Rapids: Eerdmans, 2013], 109, emphasis original)—I remain convinced that it does include a reference to the male-female sexual encounter, especially in light of the theme of nakedness and shame in Genesis 2:25.

5. Kevin DeYoung, *What Does the Bible Really Teach about Homosexuality?* (Wheaton, IL: Crossway, 2015), 28, emphasis original.

6. The following discussion of exclusivity and permanence as two features of marriage owes much to Lee and George, *Conjugal Union*, 56–67.

7. See Steven W. Thrasher, "Master Bedroom, Extra Closet: The Truth about Gay Marriage," *Gawker*, June 19, 2013, http://gawker.com/master-bedroom-extra-closet-the-truth-about-gay-marri-514348538 (accessed February 10, 2017): "The Gay Couples Study out of San Francisco State University—which, in following over 500 gay couples over many years is the largest on-going study of its kind—has found that about half of all couples have sex with someone other than their partner, *with their partner knowing*" (emphasis original). See also Scott James, "Many

Successful Gay Marriages Share an Open Secret," *New York Times*, January 28, 2010, www.nytimes.com/2010/01/29/us/29sfmetro.html (accessed February 10, 2017).

8. Hanna Rosin, "The Dirty Little Secret: Most Gay Couples Aren't Monogamous," *Slate*, June 26, 2013, www.slate.com/blogs/xx_factor/2013/06/26/most_gay_couples_aren_t_monogamous_will_straight_couples_go_monogamish.html (accessed February 10, 2017).

9. See Lee and George, *Conjugal Union*, 61–67.

10. See Jennifer Roback Morse, "Why Unilateral Divorce Has No Place in a Free Society," in *The Meaning of Marriage: Family, State, Market, and Morals*, ed. Robert P. George and Jean Bethke Elshtain (Dallas: Spence, 2006), 74–99.

11. Paul Rampell, "A High Divorce Rate Means It's Time to Try 'Wedleases,'" *Washington Post*, August 4, 2013, www.washingtonpost.com/opinions/a-high-divorce-rate-means-its-time-to-try-wedleases/2013/08/04/f2221c1c-f89e-11e2-b018-5b8251f0c56e_story.html (accessed February 10, 2017).

12. Sam Allberry, *Is God Anti-Gay? And Other Questions about Homosexuality, the Bible and Same-Sex Attraction*, rev. ed. (Epsom, Surrey, UK: Good Book Company, 2015), 18.

13. Numerous social scientific studies done between the 1970s and early 2000s suggested that, on average, couples were 33 percent more likely to divorce if they had previously cohabitated. It must be acknowledged, however, that some more recent studies challenge this assumption, especially by accounting for the age of partners when they either begin cohabitating or get married (see Arielle Kuperberg, "Does

Premarital Cohabitation Raise Your Risk of Divorce?"
Council on Contemporary Families, March 10, 2014,
https://contemporaryfamilies.org/cohabitation-divorce
-brief-report (accessed February 10, 2017).

## Chapter 5: What Is Sex For?

1. For the full text of the ruling, see "*Obergefell et al v. Hodges*,"
   Argued April 28, 2015—Decided June 26, 2015, https://
   www.supremecourt.gov/opinions/14pdf/14-556_3204.pdf
   (accessed February 10, 2017).

2. E. J. Graff, "Same-Sex Marriage Is a Radical Feminist
   Idea," *American Prospect*, June 28, 2012, http://prospect.org/
   article/same-sex-marriage-radical-feminist-idea (accessed
   February 10, 2017); cited in Ryan Anderson, "Marriage:
   What It Is, Why It Matters, and the Consequences
   of Redefining It," Heritage Foundation, March 11,
   2013, www.heritage.org/marriage-and-family/report/
   marriage-what-it-why-it-matters-and-the-consequences
   -redefining-it (accessed February 10, 2017).

3. Nancy Jo Sales, "Tinder and the Dawn of the 'Dating
   Apocalypse,'" *Vanity Fair*, September 2015, www.vanityfair
   .com/culture/2015/08/tinder-hook-up-culture-end-of
   -dating (accessed February 10, 2017).

4. For a rich, reflective analysis of our hypersexualized culture,
   see Jonathan Grant, *Divine Sex: A Compelling Vision for
   Christian Relationships in a Hypersexualized Age* (Grand Rapids:
   Brazos, 2015).

5. See Donna Freitas, *Sex and the Soul: Juggling Sexuality,*

*Spirituality, Romance, and Religion on America's College Campuses*, rev. ed. (2008; repr., New York: Oxford University Press, 2015).

6. See J. Budziszewski, *On the Meaning of Sex* (Wilmington, DE: ISI, 2012), 17–33.

7. I'm indebted for many of these insights to Sherif Girgis, Ryan T. Anderson, and Robert P. George, *What Is Marriage? Man and Woman: A Defense* (New York: Encounter, 2012), esp. 23–36; Patrick Lee and Robert P. George, *Conjugal Union: What Marriage Is and Why It Matters* (Cambridge: Cambridge University Press, 2014); and Budziszewski, *On the Meaning of Sex*.

8. See William M. Struthers, *Wired for Intimacy: How Pornography Hijacks the Male Brain* (Downers Grove, IL: InterVarsity, 2010).

9. Aristotle, *Nicomachean Ethics*, 8.11, http://classics.mit.edu/Aristotle/nicomachaen.8.viii.html (accessed February 10, 2017).

10. Wendell Berry, "Sex, Economy, Freedom, and Community," in *Sex, Economy, Freedom & Community: Eight Essays* (New York: Pantheon, 1992), 142. The entire essay repays a careful reading.

11. C. S. Lewis, *The Lion, the Witch and the Wardrobe* (1950; repr., New York: HarperCollins, 1994), 86.

12. Ironically, as our culture has severed the public consequence of sex (i.e., children) from the private act of sex, we've felt the need to compensate somehow by putting this private act (i.e., sex) on public display in all sorts of unseemly ways.

13. By "win," I mean to say there are very real and substantial social benefits to marriage. For a succinct elaboration of these, grounded in careful social scientific research, see Girgis, Anderson, and George, *What Is Marriage?* 42–46.

14. Lauren Sandler, "The Economic Reason for Having Just One Child," *Time*, June 11, 2013, http://ideas.time.com/2013/06/11/the-economic-reason-for-having-just-one-child (accessed February 10, 2017).

15. For a judicious assessment of the Protestant tradition's handling of the issue of contraception, see Kathryn D. Blanchard, "The Gift of Contraception: Calvin, Barth, and a Lost Protestant Conversation," *Journal of the Society of Christian Ethics* 27.1 (Spring/Summer 2007): 225–49.

16. Christopher Ash, *Marriage: Sex in the Service of God* (Vancouver, BC: Regent College Publishing, 2003).

17. William H. Willimon, "Children: The Blessed Burden," *Duke Divinity School Review* 45.1 (Winter 1980): 42, https://archive.org/stream/dukedivinityscho45duke/dukedivinityscho45duke_djvu.txt (accessed February 10, 2017).

18. Ibid.

## Chapter 6: Friendship, Celibacy, and Same-Sex Relationships

1. Wesley Hill, *Spiritual Friendship: Finding Love in the Church as a Gay Christian* (Grand Rapids: Brazos, 2015), 19.

2. Ibid., 19–20.

3. I am indebted to Wesley Hill's own masterful reflections in his *Spiritual Friendship*.

4. See Jana Marguerite Bennett, *Water Is Thicker Than Blood: An Augustinian Theology of Marriage and Singleness* (New York: Oxford University Pres, 2008).

5. Hill, *Spiritual Friendship*, 20, emphasis original.

6. Ibid., 21–22, emphasis original.

7. Wesley Hill, "Why Can't Men Be Friends?" *Christianity Today* 58.7 (September 16, 2014): 38, www.christianitytoday .com/ct/2014/september/why-cant-men-be-friends-wesley -hill-friendship.html (accessed February 10, 2017).

8. Ibid.

## Chapter 7: Homeward Bound

1. Cited in Tyler O'Neil, "Christians Are Following Secular Trends in Premarital Sex, Cohabitation Outside of Marriage, Says Dating Site Survey," *Christian Post*, January 27, 2014, www.christianpost.com/news/christians-are -following-secular-trends-in-premarital-sex-cohabitation -outside-of-marriage-says-dating-site-survey-113373 (accessed February 10, 2017).

2. Melinda Selmys, *Sexual Authenticity: An Intimate Reflection on Homosexuality and Catholicism* (Huntington, IN: Our Sunday Visitor, 2009), 155.

3. Ibid., 153.

4. J. R. R. Tolkien, *The Return of the King: Being the Third Part of The Lord of the Rings* (1955; repr., New York: Houghton Mifflin, 2012), 957.

5. Wesley Hill, *Washed and Waiting: Reflections on Christian Faithfulness & Homosexuality*, rev. ed. (2010; repr., Grand Rapids: Zondervan, 2016), 63–64.

## Conclusion: Casting Vision with Joy, Tears, and Hope

1. Carl R. Trueman, "We Need to Win the Aesthetic, Not the Argument," *First Things*, October 12, 2016, www .firstthings.com/blogs/firstthoughts/2016/10/we-need-to -win-the-aesthetic-not-the-argument (accessed February 10, 2017).

2. See Art Lindsley, "The Importance of Imagination for C. S. Lewis and for Us," *C. S. Lewis Institute Report* (Summer 2001), www.cslewisinstitute.org/webfm_ send/277 (accessed February 10, 2017).

3. Quoted in Justin Buckley Dyer and Micah J. Watson, *C. S. Lewis on Politics and the Natural Law* (New York: Cambridge University Press, 2016); original quote from C. S. Lewis, "Sometimes Fairy Stories May Say Best What's to Be Said," in *Of Other Worlds: Essays and Stories* (New York: Harcourt, Brace, Jovanovich, 1982), 42.

## Appendix 1: Four Core Scriptural Convictions

1. Kevin DeYoung, *What Does the Bible Really Teach about Homosexuality?* (Wheaton, IL: Crossway, 2015), 74.

2. DeYoung, *What Does the Bible Really Teach about Homosexuality?* 90–91. This comment is made in a discussion about how this sort of critique can be unfairly leveled against the historic Christian position on same-sex practice. DeYoung helpfully examines the faulty reasoning in this approach (90–95).

## Appendix 2: Bent Sexuality

1. This chapter, written by my friend and colleague Dr. Joel Willitts, began life as a message he preached as part of a sermon series on the theme of mere sexuality at Calvary Memorial Church in Oak Park, Illinois, where I serve as pastor.

2. Cited in "The 1 in 6 Statistic: Yes, It's Hard to Believe," https://1in6.org/the-1-in-6-statistic (accessed February 10, 2017); see D. Finkelhor et al., "Sexual Abuse in a National Survey of Adult Men and Women: Prevalence, Characteristics, and Risk Factors," *Child Abuse & Neglect* 14 (1990): 19–28.

3. Dan Allender, "Men & Sexual Abuse: Hope for Wounded Hearts," Focus on the Family, podcast audio, June 27, 2012, www.focusonthefamily.com/media/daily-broadcast/ men-and-sexual-abuse-hope-for-wounded-hearts-pt1 (accessed February 10, 2017); see also Dan Allender, *The Wounded Heart: Hope for Adult Victims of Childhood Sexual Abuse* (Colorado Springs: NavPress, 2008), 47; Christine A. Courtois, *Healing the Incest Wound: Adult Survivors in Therapy* (New York: Norton, 2010), 22; Andrew J. Schmutzer, ed., *The Long Journey Home: Understanding and Ministering to the Sexually Abused* (Eugene, OR: Wipf & Stock, 2011), 5.

4. John Barr and Jeff Goodman, "Former Louisville Recruit about His Visit: 'It Was Like I Was in a Strip Club,'" ESPN, October 20, 2015, http://espn.go.com/espn/otl/ story/_/id/13927159/former-louisville-cardinals-basketball -players-recruits-acknowledge-stripper-parties-minardi-hall (accessed February 10, 2017).

5. Dan Allender, *The Healing Path: How the Hurts in Your Past Can Lead You to a More Abundant Life* (Colorado Springs: WaterBrook, 1999), 8–14.

6. Ibid., 14.

7. See Curt Thompson, *The Soul of Shame: Retelling the Stories We Believe about Ourselves* (Downers Grove, IL: InterVarsity, 2015), 47–48.

8. I heard this quote in a recording of a Dan Allender seminar, "Redeeming Sexuality."

9. Joy A. Schroeder, "Sexual Abuse and a Theology of Embodiment: Incarnated Healing," in *The Long Journey Home*, ed. Schmutzer, 193.

10. Bessel van der Kolk, *The Body Keeps the Score: Brain, Mind, and Body in the Healing of Trauma* (New York: Viking Penguin, 2014), 3.

11. Notable exceptions have been Dallas Willard, *The Spirit of the Disciplines: Understanding How God Changes Lives* (New York: HarperCollins, 1988), and Curt Thompson's recent work in his two books, *Anatomy of the Soul: Surprising Connections between Neuroscience and Spiritual Practices That Can Transform Your Life and Relationships* (Carol Stream, IL: SaltRiver, 2010), and *The Soul of Shame: Retelling the Stories We Believe about Ourselves*; see also Victor Copan, *Changing Your Mind: The Bible, the Brain, and Spiritual Growth* (Eugene, OR: Wipf & Stock, 2016).

12. It's worth at least mentioning that the passage 7:53–8:11 is set off with double brackets in modern versions of the Bible because the earliest Greek manuscripts of John do not contain the story. So while in all likelihood this

story is not original to John's gospel, the story has every indication of being a genuine Jesus story. It fits John's theological outlook and has a powerful message worthy of deep reflection.

13. Quote famously made by German New Testament scholar Ernst Käsemann ("The Beginnings of Christian Theology," in *New Testament Questions of Today*, trans. W. J. Montague [London: SCM, 1969], 102).

14. M. Scott Peck, *People of the Lie: The Hope for Healing Human Evil* (New York: Touchstone, 1983), 42.

15. Ibid., 43.

16. Wendell Berry, *Remembering: A Novel* (San Francisco: North Point, 1988).

# Real Christian

## Bearing the Marks of Authentic Faith

*Todd Wilson*

The evangelical church is home to many who claim to follow Christ but who show little evidence of a truly transformed life. Todd Wilson's *Real Christian: Bearing the Marks of Authentic Faith* biblically defines what it means to be a true Christian, calling readers to look at their own lives and diagnose where they aren't living authentically for God. With a prophetic voice, Wilson looks at how we deceive ourselves into thinking we are really living for God through believing the right things or doing lots of spiritual activities. In contrast, real Christians are marked by these key qualities: humility, meekness, contrition, wholeness, and hunger. And all of these qualities culminate in the mark of marks—namely, love.

To help in distinguishing genuine faith from counterfeit spirituality, Wilson draws on the Gospels, the writings of Paul, and the insights of theologian Jonathan Edwards to help readers understand the necessary marks of an authentic, transformed life—marks that show evidence of a new heart and bear spiritual fruit through the work of the Holy Spirit.

*Available in stores and online!*

# The Pastor Theologian

## Resurrecting an Ancient Vision

*Gerald Hiestand and Todd Wilson*

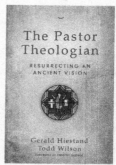

Pastoral ministry today is often ruled by an emphasis on short-sighted goals, pragmatic results, and shallow thinking. Unfortunately, those in the academy tend to have the opposite problem, failing to connect theological study to the pressing issues facing the church today. Contemporary evangelicalism has lost sight of the inherent connection between pastoral leadership and theology. This results in theologically anemic churches and ecclesial anemic theologies.

Todd Wilson and Gerald Hiestand contend that among a younger generation of evangelical pastors and theologians, there is a growing appreciation for the native connection between theology and pastoral ministry. At the heart of this recovery of a theological vision for ministry is the re-emergence of the role of the "pastor theologian."

*The Pastor Theologian* shows how individual pastors—given their unique calling and gift set—can best embody this age-old vocation in the twenty-first century. They present three models that combine theological study and practical ministry to the church:

- the local theologian—a pastor theologian who ably services the theological needs of a local congregation
- the popular theologian—a pastor theologian who writes theology to a wider lay audience
- the ecclesial theologian—a pastor theologian who writes theology to other theologians and scholars

Raising the banner for the pastor as theologian, this book invites an emerging generation of theologians and pastors to reimagine the pastoral vocation along theological lines and to identify with one of the above models of the pastor theologian.

*Available in stores and online!*

ZONDERVAN®
.com